72 LESSONS FROM THE SKY

CESSNA 172

FLETCHER MCKENZIE

SSP

This edition published 2023 by Squabbling Sparrows Press

ISBN 978-1-9911576-4-5 (Paperback)
ISBN 978-0-9951369-0-8 (Ebook)

Published by Squabbling Sparrows Press
PO Box 4213, Marewa, Napier 4143
New Zealand

Squabbling Sparrows Press

ALSO BY FLETCHER MCKENZIE

LESSONS FROM THE SKY

STORIES & LESSONS FROM
FROM CESSNA 172 PILOTS

"More pilots over the years have earned their wings in a 172 than any other aircraft in the world."

Doug May
    Textron Aviation

To my beloved daughter, who lights up my world. May this book inspire you to dream big and never stop flying and learning. You are the reason for my joy and the reason I wrote Lessons From The Sky. I love you now and always, and I remain your biggest fan.

Dad.

CONTENTS

FOREWORD
WARREN SATTLER

As a young boy, I'd always been interested in aviation, especially with an uncle who trained to fly in World War II. But it wasn't until one Easter weekend that I took a scenic flight above Rotorua, New Zealand's adventure playground. Even though I didn't feel particularly well afterwards, I enjoyed it enough to say to myself, "Let's give this a go."

I learned to fly in a Victor 100. Back then, the Cessna 172 was an aircraft you aspired to fly, and well known for their smooth throaty sound.

It was never my intention to do a PPL, but I was drawn to flying. I have now chalked up some 35,000 hours GA (General Aviation) flying. I have flown all the Cessna's — the 150, the 152, in fact, most Cessna models, including the 336, the 337, the 177, the 182, right through to the 404s and 420s. You name it, I've flown it. I was also the first person in New Zealand to fly a tail dragger conversion 152.

After finishing my PPL, I finally flew the 172. Unsurprisingly, my interest in flying continued to develop, and I completed my commercial licence. Then my instrument rating. Onto my multi-engine rating, and finally my instructor rating.

Just as I completed my training, there was a major upheaval within NAC and Air New Zealand, and they stopped flying the Fokker Friendships. As a result, the hiring of pilots stopped for seven years. So I kept instructing in Cessna's.

The 172 is probably the safest airplane I have flown, particularly from a flight training point of view. Saying this in tongue in cheek, "If I was going to crash in anything, let it be at 172". An extraordinarily flexible aircraft, with very good low-speed characteristics, so therefore very "survivable". By the time you actually need to touchdown, you're going pretty damn slow. Far better to go in with something like a 172, than some of the other aircraft I can think of...

The 172 is both easy to fly, but difficult as well, because of coordination in particular, from a training point of view, from slow speed to high speed. The interaction between ailerons and rudder, I think, hones the student pilot to quite a high level, if they master it. Occasionally I fly with someone new and I think, "Oh my god, here we go again" with all this aileron, waggling and adverse yaw. From a training point of view, it's a forgiving airplane, flexible, with great manoeuvrability.

It's been interesting watching the changes that Cessna has made over the stalling characteristics. Some of the earlier Cessna's would bite nicely on the stall, particularly the 152s. They'd bite superbly, with a solid wing drop stall. The biggest change was to the L or the N, which had a droop leading edge that had a profound effect on the aeroplane. It dropped the stall speed quite considerably, and the manoeuvrability went up.

I miss is the older model Cessna's with 40 degrees of flap. Because of several accidents in the United States, they bought it back to 30 degrees. As an old hand, I can say that the 40 degrees gave it a real edge. In any precision short field landing competition, give me a 40 degree flap Cessna.

Over the years, I've seen the engine develop from the 145, 150, 160 horsepower, then conversions to the 180 horsepower, the XP 195 and eventually 210 horsepower. All in the same airframe. How versatile is that!

The book says you don't sideslip a Cessna with the flaps down. You can do it, but it does blanket the tailplane and your controls. Not good for students. Particularly in the R and the S models. Doing a sideslip very clearly much prefers going to the left than the right. From time to time I've side slipped with full flap, but you need to make sure you've got plenty of speed to do so.

The R and the S models have very few vices. To the extent that if you want to do a decent wind drop stall, you've got to work on it to get those. From a training point of view, with two of you in the cockpit, it's a docile aeroplane. Increasing the gross weight, with a bit of an aft C of G, it will exhibit the characteristics of a typical airplane and it will drop over quite nicely.

I've flown many Cessna's, the Cardinal, 206 and twins, 404s etc from New Zealand across a lot of water — Vanuatu (very interesting flying!), and Australia. The smallest airplane I ferried was a 152 to New Caledonia. I've had a lot of firsts. I flew the first Cessna 162 in New Zealand, the first person to have a Partnavia rating, which I gave myself. That was fairly interesting. If I walked out any flight line and they said, have a pick of whatever's there, it would always be a Cessna for me.

Maintenance, maintenance, maintenance. At the end of the day, aeroplanes are a collection of bits. One of the biggest downfall of the early Lycoming powerplant was camshaft wear. Since tappets have gone in, they have been magnificent. We have had teardown reports after engines have gone back to the factory. The camshafts are in a state where they could literally go straight back into the aircraft and be used again. We don't skimp on maintenance and, as a result, we're regularly getting 4,000 hours out of our engines. Our oil analysis has been a boon, and it's been very useful on the journey. The role of tappets has put the engines into a completely different league.

We were one of the first flying schools in New Zealand to get the 172 diesel engine conversion. We had five converted 172s — a total of 155 horsepower burning 22-23 litres an hour. At 75% power, sea level power can be maintained to 18,000 feet. It is a joy to climb to 10,000 feet. The old 172 really climbs. We watch the other 172s with their normal engine, falling off at 5,000 and 6,000 feet. We hold 800 feet a minute to 10,000 feet, which is quite something.

It's true that the engines are not cheap. I did a comparison over 3,000 hours (before the 2022 Ukraine war) in the 172-S. We were looking at NZ$300,000 in terms of fuel costs. With the diesel conversion, you're looking at NZ$105,000. Maintenance may be more expensive, as there are specific checks on hours done. But you have a lot of extra money for maintenance with the NZ$200,000 in fuel savings.

When you look at a Cessna 172, then examine other similar aircraft, you'll see these designs all originated from the Cessna — the high wing, the form, the structure. So many look like a Cessna. From the Jabiru to the Tecnam, I look at them and I say, well; I wonder where that concept came from. The Cessna 172 is damn hard to beat.

Warren Sattler
A-Cat Examiner

35,000 hours of flight instruction experience and as an A Cat Instructor with General Aviation flight testing privileges. He is committed and dedicated to training pilots, seeing them succeed in their airline careers. Warren was awarded a Life Membership of the Aviation Industry Association in 2010.

INTRODUCTION
CAPTAIN JOHN MAZUR

My love for aviation started when I was an elementary school student, riding along with my dad in his friend's airplane. I was hooked. While still in high school, in Mt. Carmel, Pennsylvania I paid for my private pilot's certificate with my summer job, learning to fly a Cessna 150 A. I flew from a grass strip in the anthracite coal area, a hard coal place. Money was scarce, and the Cessna 150 was affordable with its small engine. Interestingly, I had to hitch-hike to the airport for flying lessons since I wasn't yet old enough to drive a car.

The first time I saw a Cessna 172, I thought here's the same airplane, but bigger, meaning I could take more friends. I was excited. I thought this was the perfect airplane.

I enlisted in the Air National Guard hoping to fly for the military. After Vietnam, our military forces were being reduced and no pilot slots were available. I became an airplane engine mechanic for the EC 121 Constellation. In the military, I learned about Embry-Riddle Aeronautical University and decided to continue my education in Daytona Beach, earning a degree in Aeronautical Studies. It is one of the most renowned aviation universities in the world, with several campuses in the USA, in China and in more than 130 locations all over the world. What is their choice as the most efficient and safest airplane? Due to the high number of hours they fly versus the very low number of incidents or accidents, it would have to considered the safest plane in the world. They're using the 172 as their primary, instrument and commercial trainer.

Overall, the 172 is an awesome airplane. Parts are available everywhere, as are experienced mechanics. It's affordable to own and operate compared to some other aircraft. It's just a perfect personal airplane. While at the aviation university, I completed my commercial, instrument and CFI (Certified Flight Instructor) ratings in a 172.

After graduation, I got my first job establishing a flight school with Beechcraft, setting up their Beech Aero Clubs and Flight Training Centers. I worked with a nearby university to establish a fully accredited Aviation Degree program. Due to making headlines with the university and flight school's success, I earned a personal interview with Olivia Beech, who offered me the opportunity to do the same with their Aero Club Flight Centers nationwide.

One of my students owned an old 1963 Cessna 172, and I was instructing him in it. We were in Charleston, West Virginia, a mountainous area, with not a lot of flat landing spots. He said, if I ever wanted to use the airplane, just gas it up you're welcome to it. I'd often find myself night flying over the highest mountains in the eastern United States. Bad weather would force commercial airlines to go around, on missed approaches, while I was flying overhead back to Daytona Beach, to visit friends in the 172. It is such a reliable airplane. One late night flight I was in turbulence over mountains at the highest Minimum Safe Altitude (MSA) in the east, almost at the aircraft's limits and it handled it very well. It's a very stable flyer to learn and enjoy cross-country experience flying over the mountains.

I have great respect for Cessna 172. There's a reason why it's the most popular airplane in the world. I have been able to fly many great aircraft over my career, from light planes, and corporate jets, to heavy aircraft, and the 172. It is one of the most desirable airplanes anyone can fly and own. In my opinion, there is nothing else that can beat it. My background includes 32,000 plus hours and I appreciate what the 172 offers. That should mean a lot.

The high wing of the 172 gives all occupants a great view. It's easy to look around and see where you are. It has the added bonus of when you're on the ground there's somewhere to stand outside in the shade when it's sunny, or to protect you from the rain when you're unloading bags or doing preflight checks. It's easier to get into than most low wing airplanes and there's enough room inside to take friends for joy rides, travelling to places too far to drive to. With its large windows, you sit high in the airplane, and have more visibility than almost any other airplane that I have flown. A docile and forgiving aircraft, it's also great for learning to land with its forgiving spring steel landing gear. A requirement as beginner pilots may tend to hit the runway harder when initially learning proper landing technique.

It's advanced enough to take friends on a cross-country flight at a decent speed. A Bonanza or a jet can get you to places faster but the enjoyment of flying is just being in the air, seeing what you can see with your own eyes, greatly expanding your personal horizon. I take friends up frequently to enjoy a beautiful sunrise or sunset.

I became a corporate jet pilot, first flying a Westwind 1124 jet. I have also flown Lears, Falcons and Gulfstreams. Typically, corporate pilots don't fly as much as airline pilots, so I started a banner towing business. Being in a mountainous area with most of the towns in a river valley, my idea was to fly over the American football games at West Virginia University of Morgantown, and Marshall University in Huntington. I would also fly over the river valleys where the houses were lined up along the sides of mountains. Families could look straight out from the houses on the hillside, and I'd be in my 172 towing banners, at their eye level. The 172 is enjoyable and fun to fly, even when towing political banners.

After being hired by US Airways, I bought my first home in New

Hampshire, with my new bride Darlene. We chose to be based nearby in Boston. Within a year, Darlene became a Flight Attendant for the same airline. I started as a B-727 Flight engineer, but within months I become a DC-9 First Officer. My first Captain rating was in the Boeing 737, which I refer to as the 172 of the airline world. Both are the world's most popular airplanes of the airline and general aviation aircraft categories respectively. Additionally, I have additional type ratings in various large Airbus and Boeing airliners. US Airways has since merged with American Airlines.

Commercial flying is great, but I missed light airplane flying, so I started an aero club in Nashua, New Hampshire. It was the busiest general aviation airport in the northeast United States, located about a 45 minute drive northwest of Boston. My first advertisement read, "Flight instructor starting private pilot ground school and Aero Club. Enjoy saving costs while learning to fly." I named it Nashua Flyers, and bought my first 172. People showed up! I didn't charge much, as the goal was to share the joy of flying. Forty years later I'm told that original aircraft still exists in Nashua. I don't know of another airplane that would be able to last that long with so many different people flying. It's a durable, well-designed airplane that is safe, economical and a gentle trainer.

I was able to spin a 172, you can't do that in a 182 or any Piper's I know of. Spins are a required maneuver to become a certified flight instructor with the FAA. With the 172 design, it's great, for that exhilarating maneuver. Since one can't spin in many other airplanes most flight schools almost have to have 172s for their CFI training. When I first learned to fly, spin training was a requirement for even the Private Pilot Certificate.

I've flown a lot of hours and there are a lot of things that have happened. I've never had an accident or incident breaking rules or violating the law. I believe it's because of learning to fly in a 172 has created great habit patterns. Over the years, I've had several engine failures, and I've had people trying to break into our cockpit. I've had a baby delivered on board, so we landed with one more passenger than we took off with. I have had a lot of other things happen in the airline and corporate flying world as well. Even if I were piloting the space shuttle, I still wouldn't have outgrown what I've learned in the 172.

Although flying a 172 in 45-knot winds is probably not the best idea. I found I could do it safely with my experience and my understanding of the aircraft. But I don't recommend trying it!

I have owned six different airplane types and have never lost money on a 172. Buying brand new is expensive. But a used one, if well taken care of, can be as reliable as a brand new aircraft. I've made money on every 172 I've had. I also have had Beechcraft and Piper airplanes. When I was a student at Embry Riddle, I bought an Aeronca Chief. It is similar to a tandem seating Champ, a tailwheel and fabric airplane but the Chief has side-by-side seating. Interestingly, all my 172s have outperformed my bank investments so I have had the added benefit of being able to fly and enjoy these 172 investments.

If you take care of it while operating the 172, you will have the enjoyment of a beautiful (no matter how old it is), well-running, flying airplane, and you will get the value back when you sell. The better you take care of it, the more desirable and valuable the airplane will be.

There's a plaque on the wall at home, "A superior pilot uses his superior judgment to avoid situations requiring the use of his superior skills." The habit patterns and skills I have learned on the 172, I am able to apply to my multi-engine and jet flying. I've had numerous situations, engine failures, and all sorts of incidents but because of what I learned in the 172, safety has carried right over. Piloting an airplane is the same or very similar in any type airplane you're flying. If you pull back on the control yoke, the houses get smaller, if you push forward the houses get bigger. Learning to fly in a 172 can safely build greatly intuitive safety skills.

I have found the positive stability of the airplane is unmatched compared to most aircraft. If you have enough altitude and you did get into a stall or spin, just let go of everything, and the 172 will find its way back to straight and level. Even with no power on the engine, with its positive stability it will turn itself right side up into a glide. There are just so many good things to say about the airplane.

I have plenty of experience and ratings, and yet I learn every single day. The airline that employs me to teach their captains and pilots, think I know almost everything. However, If I thought that, I would be dangerous. Among the best advice I can offer, is for you to know your limits and abide by them. Never stop learning. Adding additional ratings is a great way to stay proficient. A true professional is always learning and always improving.

I know you will enjoy flying the 172. Happy Landings!

Captain John Mazur

A private pilot whilst still in high school, he then became an airplane engine mechanic with the Air National Guard. He attended Embry-Riddle Aeronautical University, becoming a flight instructor and flight school operator, charter pilot, airplane banner towing pilot, corporate jet pilot, airline pilot, an Airline Instructor and CRM Safety course developer, a participant in NASA's Pilot Fatigue research. John lives in Spruce Creek Fly-In, a flying community in a home with a hangar attached and a taxiway behind. His wife Darlene is a flight attendant. Their sons, Matthew and Johnny, are both commercially certificated instrument and multi-engine flight instructors. John's picture hangs in the Air and Space Museum in Washington, DC, as part of America by Air display. He was also awarded the Wright Brothers Master Pilot Award. He has over 5000+ Cessna 172 hours.

PROLOGUE

"If the engine stops for any reason, you are due to tumble, and that's all there is to it."

Clyde Cessna

In 1911, a Kansas farmer breathed life into a fragile-looking wood and fabric aircraft and became the first person to fly between the Mississippi River and the Rocky Mountains. His name was Clyde Cessna and for over eight decades, his name has been synonymous with the world's top selling aircraft.

Inspired by a 1911 flying exhibition in Oklahoma City, U.S.A., Clyde Cessna's greatest wish was to fly. Fuelled by a passion for flight, his inspiration was the American version of the Bleriot XI, and he created his first monoplane using linen and spruce. Known as the "Silverwing," it was powered by a 40 hp Elbridge 4 cylinder motor. His first flight attempt ended in a ground loop, costing him US$100 in repairs.

After twelve more attempted flights, Clyde's aircraft bounced and then flew, but only for a short time. After crashing into trees whilst attempting to turn the aircraft, he is quoted as saying, "I'm going to fly this thing, then I'm going to set it afire and never have another thing to do with aeroplanes!".

It was in Oklahoma, where he tested his early planes on the salt flats. Between 1912 and 1915, he created several monoplane designs, powered by an Anzani 6-cylinder engine, providing between 40 and 60 hp. He also opened a flight school that ran out of his factory.

Clyde Cessna partnered with Lloyd Stearman and Walter Beech to create the Travel Air Manufacturing Company in 1925. As the company's president, it soon became one of the leading US aircraft manufacturers because of Clyde's advanced design ideas. Several years later, he proposed a monoplane design without wing struts. When his (now famous) associates dismissed it, he left and built the cantilevered wing monoplane, the Comet.

That small aircraft company set out to do what others said could not be done — building a monoplane that used a wing without supporting struts or braces. The Cessna All Purpose aircraft took flight on August 13, 1927. With this, the aviation world and industry changed forever and Clyde Cessna's cantilever design has been the ongoing standard ever since.

Several other aircraft designs took flight, including the AW, CW-6 and DC-6 in 1929. That same year Cessna collaborated with his son, Eldon, and together they created the CR-series racing aircraft, which was how the company survived trading through the Great Depression. Their financial respite was short-lived, and the Cessna Aircraft Company eventually declared bankruptcy in 1931.

In 1934, with the hard work of his nephews, Dwane and Dwight Wallace (who later took over the company) persuaded Clyde to reopen the company. They introduced the efficient four-seat C-34, a high-winged aircraft with a strutless cantilever wing design, featuring Cessna's first flaps. A racing favourite and considered nearly impossible to beat.

Clyde retired from the company in 1936, and passed away on November 20, 1954, aged 74. His legacy lives on. Posthumously inducted into the National Aviation Hall of Fame in 1978, and into the International Air & Space Hall of Fame in 1983, the Cessna name will always be linked to the skies.

Whilst many assume that the story of the 172 starts Clyde, it was his nephew, Dwane Wallace, who rescued the company from bankruptcy, with the launch of the C-34, kick-starting a new era of all-metal construction and mass production. This era helped create a new market for personal and business light aviation transportation. Cessna became a global leader and build over 100,000 aircraft while Wallace steered the company. There was a constant refinement and new markets forged, including light jets.

It's hard to find any modern day pilot who has not logged a few hours in a Cessna 172 (also known as the Skyhawk). Originally, the Cessna 172 was called just that — the Cessna 172. In 1960, the name Skyhawk came about with the release of the 172B. There was an option for a standard package, or a deluxe option package — the Skyhawk — which came with extra equipment and full exterior paint. Over time, the Skyhawk name stuck and is now refers to the entire Cessna 172 fleet. The Skyhawk piston is the most popular single engine aircraft ever built, with a reputation for being the ultimate training aircraft. Boasting a slow landing speed and a lenient stall, these characteristics make it a favourite with most flight training schools.

The 172 Skyhawk has changed little from its original simple, rugged, and reliable 1956 design, still based on the Cessna 170, but with tricycle landing gear replacing the conventional tailwheel arrangement.

The Cessna 172 holds the World Record for Flight Endurance to this day. The first 172 to hold it was owned by Jim Heth and Bill Burkhart, who took to the skies over Dallas, Texas in August 1958. Dubbed 'The Old Scotchman', they stayed in the air for 50 days.

Then, on December 4, 1958, Robert Timm and John Cook left the ground, landing 64 days, 22 hours and 19 minutes later, on February 4, 1959, at the McCarran Airfield in Las Vegas, Nevada, breaking the record and raising much needed funds for the Damon Runyon Cancer Fund.

The governments of Austria, Greece, Singapore, Iraq, and Chile have purchased various civilian variants of Cessna 172 Skyhawk for their military, using the aircraft for a number of different roles, including training. In 1964, the U.S. Air Force ordered 855 stock standard Skyhawks, renaming it the T-41 Mescalero. Both academies of the Air Force and Navy used the T-41 to train their pilots, while the U.S. Army utilised it for reconnaissance. Only phased out in 1993.

In 1987, at the height of the Cold War, a teenaged West German pilot, Mathias Rust, flew a Cessna 172 750km into the Soviet Union to promote world peace. In his French-built (Reims) Cessna, Rust evaded the world's most formidable air defence system, made up of thousands of anti-aircraft missile launchers, and landed on a bridge on the edge of Moscow's Red Square. He flew low to evade Russian air defence radar. However, a MiG fighter approached him and mistook him for a Soviet training plane. The Soviet Union's jet fighters found it too difficult to match the Cessna's slower speed. Rust stated that he wanted to land the plane in the middle of Red Square in order to make a statement but the landmark was full of people, so he chose a four-lane bridge next to St Basil's Cathedral, circled around and touched down.

The Soviets arrested Rust, and found him guilty of hooliganism, disregard of aviation laws, and for breaching the Soviet border. President Gorbachev used the opportunity to rid himself of military officials and in 1988, following the signing of a non-proliferation treaty by Reagan and Gorbachev, Rust was released as a gesture of goodwill after serving 14 months. Rust's Cessna is now on display in Germany's Deutches Technikmuseum.

June 12th 2020, saw the 65th anniversary of the Cessna Skyhawk's first flight. Since the production line restart in 1996, the Cessna 172 has been the top selling Light Single Engine (LSE) aircraft in the category (FAA Part 23, less than 200hp). In that time, 4 out of every 10 LSE pistons delivered have been Cessna 172s, with over 45,000 aircraft built and delivered to customers around the world.

It remains an integral part of Textron Aviation's pilot outreach efforts, with programs like Top Hawk and discovery flights for local community youth organisations.

With an impressive safety record, especially when compared to the industry average. Statistically, the Cessna 172's fatal accident rate is 0.56 per 100,000 hours. This is about half of the industry average rate of 1.2-1.4. Former Flying Magazine Editor-in-Chief Richard Collins analysed its safety record, and found the Skyhawk to be the safest single aircraft, with a nearly three times better record than the General Aviation (GA) average, thanks to its generous and well-designed flaps, landing speed, solid construction and its predictable and stable flying platform.

A story in Vector magazine (a New Zealand Civil Aviation Authority (CAA) publication) about a Cessna seat incident caught my attention. The incident occurred after the pilot pulled back the control column upon takeoff, and the aircraft seat mechanism let go. The pilot couldn't help pulling back on the control column as the seat slid back. The aircraft lurched up into a stall, luckily they were able to gain control and the aircraft landed safely without further incident. The chair rail locking device had failed.

I remember hoping that the same thing wouldn't happen to me, but interestingly I never thought to check my seat structure. Nor did I ask questions, talk to anyone or see what modifications they had completed on the 172 I usually fly. However, what I've done since reading that article was, during my preflight checks I always, without fail, gave my seat a good shake to ensure it was steady and the locking mechanism worked.

And once I was in the aircraft and buckled in, I always shook the hell out of the chair to ensure it wouldn't move on takeoff, etc.

However, I never closely examined the chair locking system or tried to understand my seat and its structure within the 172. I assumed that the club, the owners and our maintenance engineer would have looked into this.

After reading a story in the UK's CHIRP (reporting database), titled "SEAT FAILURE ON TAKEOFF", I wondered just exactly how many chair legs in the Cessna are locked in place. I assumed that all four were locked in. Next time I was at the hanger, I investigated further and upon closer inspection, I looked for the back legs and discovered that there were none. To my amazement, just one leg on the inside was used to lock the chair in place. In fact, it is a one 5mm diameter steel rod holding my 95kg frame into place. I recently flew a passenger who was 110kg (When the Cessna was designed in the 1960s, the average pilot was around 65-75kgs).

I was shocked at the one tiny leg keeping us safe. I discussed my surprise with a friend, who suggested that I should design and manufacture a device for this. No need. A quick internet search showed several seat locking devices on the market for the Cessna. I have since purchased a seat locking device for my seat, to ensure that there is one less hole in the "Swiss cheese slice" or safety layer that I need not worry about.

Since the release of my first book, *81 Lessons from the Sky*, I have had various conversations about the Cessna seat. Other pilots who went through similar occurrences were only here by sheer luck to tell their story.

During my preflight checks in a Cessna 172S (injected) for my BFR (Biennial Flight Review), I examined the seat mechanism — a very different from the 172M. It had four horizontal locking pins on each side as opposed to one on the M. It also had the tensioner (a Cessna modification which is still available at the time of writing) that ensures the seat will catch if the pins fail.

Rather than assume, I always ask someone who has flown the aircraft, in order to understand the differences, what mods are there. I make notes in "Evernote" a digital note taking system and use the callsign to ensure I do not forget what I learned and can always refer to my notes before I next fly.

The Cessna 172 is a solid classic aircraft with a long and storied history.

I have enjoyed many hours flying cross-country, flying the family around New Zealand and even streamer cutting with both wings (I love burning avgas and shredding toilet paper).

It is a well-loved, well used, reliable, and safe aircraft that are easy and enjoyable to fly. Just don't forget to check your seats!

Blue skies!

Fletcher McKenzie

HOW TO USE THIS BOOK

Each lesson has been replicated in the pilot's or crew member's words, without any editing other than minor grammatical corrections. You may notice some errors. We have purposely not amended the original reports.

A glossary of terms is included at the end of this book for your reference. Please note that this book may contain a mixture of both American English and British English, depending on who is telling the story.

If you find a term or an acronym in this book which isn't in the glossary, please email Fletcher:

fletch@avgasgroup.com

Each lesson has space for you to make your own notes if you want to. I recommend doing this to cement the learning.

Writing a short review of this book on your favourite digital platform, or on your personal blog or Facebook page, will help spread the word about aviation safety. Saving lives is the primary goal of this book.

AUSTRALIA

Flight Safety Australia:
Civil Aviation Safety Authority
(CASA)

CASA's flagship aviation safety magazine. Topical, technical, but reader-friendly, articles cover all the key aviation safety issues – safety management systems, maintenance, runway safety, human factors, airspace, training, aviation medicine and more.

Flight Safety Australia, and its predecessor the Aviation Safety Digest, have provided the Australian aviation community with credible and comprehensive aviation safety information since the early 1950s.

From its beginnings as a printed monochrome booklet published only a few times a year, Flight Safety Australia has evolved into an interactive and content-rich publication available across multiple digital platforms.

Flight Safety Australia is produced by a small, dynamic team of writers, designers and contributors based out of the Safety Promotion branch of Australia's Civil Aviation Safety Authority.

UNITED KINGDOM

Confidential Human Factors Incident
Report Programme for Aviation
(CHIRP)

Known by the acronym CHIRP, its aim is to contribute to the enhancement of flight safety in the UK commercial and general aviation industries, by providing a totally independent confidential reporting system for all individuals employed in or associated with the industries.

The Programme is available to engineers and technical staff involved with the design and manufacturing processes, flight crew members, cabin crew members, air traffic controllers, licensed engineers and maintenance/engineering personnel and individual aircraft owners/operators.

CHIRP complements the UK's CAA Mandatory Occurrence Reporting system and other formal reporting systems operated by many UK organisations, by providing a means by which individuals are able to raise safety-related issues of concern without being identified to their peer group, management, or the Regulatory Authority.

CHIRP is a totally independent programme for the collection of confidential safety data, and when appropriate, acting or advising on information gained through confidential reports. Independent advice is provided on aeromedical and Human Factors aspects of reports, involving such topics as errors, fatigue, poor ergonomics, management pressures, deficiencies in communication or team performance. The sensitivity of these topics requires that the anonymity of the reporter must be, and always has been, fully protected.

Royal Air Force Safety Centre

VISION:

A safety organisation which delivers effective Total Safety Management and leads on intelligent application of critical thinking.

MISSION:

To provide independent assurance of the RAF Safety Management System underpinning CAS' commitment to Total Safety in order to maximise the delivery of RAF capability.

UNITED STATES OF AMERICA

Aviation Safety Reporting System
(ASRS)

ASRS collects voluntarily submitted aviation safety incident/situation reports from pilots, controllers, and others. It then analyses, and responds to the voluntarily submitted aviation safety incident reports in order to lessen the likelihood of aviation accidents.

ASRS acts on the information these reports contain. It identifies system deficiencies, and issues alerting messages to persons in a position to correct them. It educates through its newsletter CALLBACK, its journal ASRS Directline and through its research studies. Its database is a public repository which serves the FAA and NASA's needs and those of other organisations world-wide which are engaged in research and the promotion of safe flight.

ASRS data are used to identify deficiencies and discrepancies in the National Aviation System (NAS) so that these can be remedied by appropriate authorities. Support policy formulation and planning for, and improvements to, the NAS and strengthen the foundation of aviation human factors safety research. This is particularly important since it is generally conceded that over two-thirds of all aviation accidents and incidents have their roots in human performance errors.

———

The Naval Safety Centre
(NAVSAFECEN)

A continuously improving command that develops leading indicators of risks and hazards to empower all Sailors, Marines, civilians and their families to embrace a proactive culture of risk identification and management to achieve zero preventable mishaps.

The Naval Safety Center was established in 1951 at the Naval Air Station, Norfolk, Virginia, it was called the U.S. Naval Aviation Safety Activity. The staff collected, evaluated and published information about aviation safety. The staff also advised the Chief of Naval Operations and the Commandant of the Marine Corps on all phases of the aviation-safety effort.

Today, the Naval Safety Center is organized into four directorates: aviation, afloat, shore, and operational risk management/expeditionary warfare. Six departments and five special staff divisions provide support to the core operations of the command. The Naval School of Aviation Safety in Pensacola, Florida, is also a NAVSAFECEN detachment consisting of civilian and military staff, which includes Marine Corps personnel. As an Echelon II command, NAVSAFECEN provides oversight of its single Echelon III command, the Naval Safety and Environmental Training Center in Norfolk, Virginia.

To preserve warfighting capability and combat lethality by identifying hazards and reducing risk to people and resources.

———

U.S. Air Force Aviation Safety

The Air Force Safety Center resides on Kirtland Air Force Base, located in the high desert of north-central New Mexico and it occupies a majority of southeast Albuquerque.

The Aviation Safety Division (SEF) consists of safety-trained professionals spanning the domain of flight. The division preserves warfighting capability by establishing Air Force aviation safety policy, promoting mishap prevention programs for all aviation assets and through the establishment of proactive safety programs. It oversees the aviation mishap investigative process, the collection and accuracy of flight safety data and the disposition of risk-mitigating actions. It provides proactive and reactive engineering and operational analyses of flight safety issues. In the 1950s when the Air Force became a separate department, the Air Force Chief of Staff designated the Office of the Inspector General to oversee all inspection and safety functions. These functions were consolidated in an inspector general group at Norton AFB, California.

On Dec. 31, 1971, the Air Force Inspection and Safety Center was activated, replacing the 1002nd Inspector General Group. The center was then divided into the Air Force Inspection Agency and the Air Force Safety Agency in August 1991. Reorganization of the air staff in 1992 created the Air Force Chief of Safety position, reporting directly to the Air Force Chief of Staff. The Chief of Safety became dual-hatted as the commander of the Air Force Safety Agency. In July 1993, the agency moved to Kirtland AFB due to the closure of Norton AFB.

Following The Blue Ribbon Panel on Aviation Safety in 1995, the Air Force Safety Center was activated on Jan. 1, 1996.

CHAPTER 1

PREPARATION

"I am going to make this thing fly? Do you hear me? I am going to make this thing fly and then I am going to set it afire and I'll never have another thing to do with airplanes. Automobiles and farm machinery – that's what I'm going to stick to."

Clyde Cessna
    After crashing his Silverwing

GET THERE 'ITIS'

CASA, 2015

After having recently achieved my private pilot's licence, I decided to take up an offer from a friend to fly to the north-western Victorian town of St. Arnaud. My mate has a property there and upon my arrival he was to pick me up from the airport. I contacted him and organised to stay for a couple of days before flying back home again.

That part of the planning was done, I booked aa Cessna 172R, with my flying school at Moorabbin Airport. I then commenced my flight planning for the trip which I was hoping to undertake the following week, weather permitting. Being my first overnight exercise, I wanted everything to go to plan. My instructor always told me that the better prepared I was for the flight the less chance there was of things going wrong (eliminate human error).

The day of the flight finally arrived and I got to Moorabbin at about 0700 for a 0930 departure. I obtained the weather report and completed my flight planning and pre-flight. Everything looked good and I departed on time with an estimated flight time of 1.5 hours. This would take me via Ballarat and Ararat then on to St. Arnaud.

The flight proceeded without a problem and I thought to myself, 'How good is this?' and that I should have got my licence years ago instead of finally doing it after reaching my so-called mid-life crisis.

On the day I planned to return to Moorabbin I first had to go into town as I did not have access to the internet. I went to an internet café, did my flight planning and submitted the plan. The weather looked CAVOK with a moderate southerly at St. Arnaud, my observation only as there is no TAF. I planned to return to Moorabbin via Bendigo, Kyneton, Kilmore and Sugarloaf reservoir. The weather for the route looked OK. There was some low cloud and reduced visibility in the late afternoon, but still above VMC, on both the area and Moorabbin forecasts. The flight home was about 1.5 hours and I planned to be back at Moorabbin at approximately 1530.

After doing my pre-flight and departing on time I was feeling pretty good about how well things had gone.

On reaching Bendigo and taking up my next heading to Kyneton, in the distance to the south I could see some of the forecast low cloud. I estimated it was far enough away not to be a problem. I reached Kyneton, then turned towards Kilmore descending from 4500ft to 3500ft still in VMC, but cloud now looking closer, but I thought, still OK to proceed.

At Kilmore I started my descent to 2500ft due to the CTA steps and lowering cloud base. Visibility was starting to reduce considerably, but I was confident I could still maintain VMC.

Approaching Yan Yean Reservoir I estimated the visibility to be about 6000 metres and I thought to myself that this was happening much earlier than expected and seemed to be worse than the forecast. Being relatively inexperienced, I pressed on thinking I could still make it back to Moorabbin. After all, it wasn't that far.

At Sugarloaf Reservoir I thought, 'I now have to make a decision whether to continue or divert,' as I could not even see the Dandenong Ranges. I decided to divert to Lilydale, gave the CTAF call and turned towards the airfield.

I had never been to Lilydale aerodrome before or even seen it, but I had the information on hand, along with Coldstream Aerodrome—pre-flight planning was paying off. In front of me I saw an airfield. I thought, 'All good, I will overfly, check the windsock then land.'

As I was overflying I saw the writing on the roof of the building—Coldstream. I did not know how I missed Lilydale but never mind; I decided to land. I flew the circuit and landed on runway 17 without a problem. I remember thinking that I was happy to be on the ground once again as the conditions had deteriorated substantially and that perhaps I had left my decision to divert too late.

After shutting down and tying the aircraft down, I contacted the flying school at Moorabbin to tell them that I would not be back as I had put down at Coldstream. They said they had been trying to ring me to let me know that the weather had been updated and that I would be better to delay my return until the next day because I would not be able to get into Moorabbin. I left the plane at Coldstream overnight and came back to the aerodrome early the next morning, but I was still unable to get out until about 1300 and was stuck on the ground until then.

Lessons Learned:

Eventually the conditions improved enough to depart and return to Moorabbin successfully. Reflecting on my flight, I was happy I had followed my instructors' advice about thorough planning, but I was disappointed with my decision to press on when I should have made the choice to divert much earlier. That saying you always hear about: 'Get there 'itis' was true. It can happen so easily, especially for the inexperienced. Lesson learnt.

NOTES:

FUEL EXHAUSTION CAUSED BY INACCURATE PLANNING

ASRS, 2015

I was Pilot In Command with one passenger making our descent on a cross country flight. It was the first time that I was flying into this airport. Although we would not be their entering airspace, I did contact ATC approach to let them know our route.

Just after making my initial inbound radio call on ZZZ's CTAF the engine lost power. By pumping the throttle I could keep the engine sputtering, but only producing 1500 RPM. Once again, I made radio contact with Approach to notify them of my situation. At that point he said that ZZZ1 would be the closest airport. I mentioned that I did not have visual contact with the airport so he gave me the heading.

We continued to maintain contact as he kept me informed as to how close I was to the airport. When I was 1000 feet AGL he reported that I was still 7 miles away. I still did not have visual contact with the airport and the upcoming terrain was hilly and filled with trees.

Just below us I spotted a picked corn field. I notified Approach that I was going to land in the field, and he told me to contact him when we landed. As I circled around to line up for landing the engine stopped completely so I made a dead stick landing in the corn field.

Neither of us were injured and there was no damage to the plane. Once we were on the ground I was unable to get Approach on the radio, so I made contact with them using my cell phone. Approach had already reported the incident and had emergency personnel on their way, who started showing up shortly.

The cause of this incident was that we simply ran out of fuel. All of the flight planning that I had done suggested that we would have 10 or more extra gallons on board. I did notice that the fuel gauges were approaching empty, but my plane is older and these gauges have not always been accurate from my past experience. At that point we were also getting relatively close to our destination so I thought we would make it.

In hindsight, it is obvious that I miscalculated my fuel needs during flight planning. I believe my main oversight came in part by using and relying too heavily on [web based flight planning program].

During the trip I made one landing at an airport on the way, which I had entered on the [web based flight planning program]. At the time, I assumed I was inserting a "stop/landing" along the way, but after talking with other pilots, I think it is considered as more of a checkpoint/fly-over point. Therefore, my extra stop resulted in extra fuel burn during takeoff and climb that wasn't included in my calculations from [the web based flight planning program].

Another calculation that I believe was incorrect is the average fuel burn for my plane. During my flight training we always used 8.5 gal/hr as an average fuel burn to do a quick check for fuel numbers. Most of my flights are short local leisure flights that are maybe 1.5 hrs max, so I generally use this number to calculate my estimated fuel needs. I also know that with full fuel I will have plenty to fly these shorter local flights, so I have grown accustomed to getting in the "ballpark" with this 8.5 gal/hr figure.

As a double check, I also used the 8.5 gal/hr figure to estimate my fuel needs for this trip as well. Unfortunately, after closely reviewing fuel records and flight times, I now believe that my plane's actual average fuel burn is more like 9.5 to 10 gal/hr, which would also help explain why it ran out before the time I expected.

Finally, another contributing factor to this incident could have been that we had a stronger than anticipated headwind. This extended our flight time which I noticed during flight, but I neglected to take action since we were getting close to our destination and I thought we still had another 30-40 minutes of fuel remaining based off of my previous calculations. Considering that I landed in a field 7 miles from the airport, a lesser headwind would have most likely resulted in the extra 4-5 minutes needed to reach the airport.

Lessons Learned:

With all that said, this incident was the result of pilot error. I miscalculated my fuel needs plain and simple. I am fortunate that this incident had a good outcome and I can now use this as a learning lesson. It has definitely shown me that accurate fuel calculations are a critical part of flight planning.

NOTES:

SOMETHING TO WATCH

CASA, 2014

I was off on a short flight with a friend from Cambridge (Hobart's GA hub) across to Bruny Island to have a look at some oyster farms. The day was clear, if a little cool, and glorious for flying. All went smoothly as we tracked south of the city of Hobart, my passenger enjoying the view after getting over a slight case of nerves. Seeing your own city from a Cessna 172 is always fun.

We landed on Bruny, enjoyed the oyster farm inspection and then took off again a couple of hours later. The plan had been to return directly to Cambridge, but we had plenty of fuel and no shortage of time, so I asked my passenger if he'd like to have a look at the D'Entrecasteaux Channel which lies between Bruny Island and the south west of mainland Tasmania. Having spent plenty of time in that area—he owned a shack a bit further down—he was very keen to see it from the air.

Why not, on such a glorious day?

I made a departure call from the Bruny strip, noting it was, 'Time two two'.

Knowing there was plenty of fuel on board, I calculated that if we were passing this point by one zero on the return, we would be well within limits of the reserves required.

We flew south west for a bit, away from home base, tracking along the coast and enjoying the view. My passenger and I were both keen divers, so we got to chatting about the spots we were seeing, what the various mountain ranges were that we could see off to the north, and how stunning this part of the world was.

Rounding South East Cape, I checked the time again to make sure all was good. Yep, two two. Plenty of time to make that one zero requirement. I decided to track a bit further up the coast, knowing that the scenery just got better and better in this remote part of the State.

Ten minutes later I figured it must be time to start heading back. I checked my watch again. Two two. That seemed oddly familiar.

'What time is it?' I asked my passenger.

'About ten to,' they answered.

For the first time in four years my watch battery had stopped.

We didn't track coastal. I simply turned the nose directly toward Cambridge and announced we'd best get ourselves back home. We still had plenty of fuel, but I'd certainly given myself a glimpse of how quickly things can go wrong.

So what should I have done? Carried a back-up watch? Nobody wears two watches. Been more aware of the time? Yes, perhaps.

What would have been far more sensible was to have planned the flight, even if just a rough, written sketch of it with some timing points written in. By just looking at my watch and expecting the one zero that would indicate a need to be at a particular point, I had no inbuilt mechanism to guard against the watch's battery life coming to an end.

If I had been noting time on a written plan, it would have very quickly been obvious when I wrote the same numbers several minutes apart.

It didn't cause a problem on that short flight where the safety parameters were wide. On a longer cross-country flight, when diversion decisions could have been affected by assumed endurance, it might quickly have become serious.

Lessons Learned:

The lesson is simple and one that we're all familiar with—plan the flight and fly the plan. It builds in safeguards against the most unlikely of errors.

<u>NOTES:</u>

DIVERT AFTER LOSING ENGINE
DUE TO POOR PLANNING

ASRS, 2016

I had received a message a day before from a friend asking if I wanted to make money for a ferry trip. With not much going on for the time being and interested in new experiences, I told him to send more details. The opportunity was to ferry the 172s to Europe.

I came in contact with the owner, and over dinner it seemed it revolved around business, with him insisting I do the trip for him listing all the positives about the adventure. The previous pilot who was supposed to conduct the trip had to cancel due to family issues and he needed a pilot at last minute. I was still skeptical and knew about the risks and asked various questions about the ordeal, but the owner reassured that with my experience I would be fine. I gave in and agreed to do the trip for him. He told me to meet him at the FBO the next morning.

Anxious as I was with little sleep, I did show up. He gave me a packet with all the details and told me I could read it in the plane when I get to cruise. Before I took off, he wanted to speak to me about the ferry tank and how to operate it.

The tank held 100 gallons of avgas along with the 53 usable in the wings. Takeoff and landing on wing tanks only and when I got up to cruise, burn off 1/3 of the left wing and then open the ferry tank valve and pull the fuel shut off valve on. The ferry tank will refuel the left wing. I filed an IFR flight plan, briefly looked at the weather, and conducted a preflight in an attempt to hurry since it was planned to be an 11-12 hour flight. My plan was that I was going to read the weather briefing in cruise in an attempt to save time.

The flight was planned from ZZZ to [the northeast coast] at 9,000 feet, with the first 7 hours going well. The smooth and VMC conditions calmed my nerves for what I was about to do. Winds were in my favor which expected to cut down on flight time. With previous altitude chamber training, I realized that I started to become mildly hypoxic. My mind was very sluggish and confused. Everything just snowballed from there. My decision was to descend to a lower altitude.

I noticed that when I was approaching the Great Lakes region, "Lake effect snow" was forming. At the time, with my inexperience with the area, I had never heard of that term. I started to feel uncomfortable and needed to do everything to get out of possible icing conditions. I spoke with each ARTCC handling me if they could provide me with updates on weather enroute to my destination. He advised there was no one else flying in my area and information was limited. I also spoke with FSS. He had reported that top were at 10,000 feet and freezing temperatures were at the surface.

My poor judgment told me to get out of the snow and climb above to be VFR on top. I slowly made my way up there. I started to notice my speed decreasing in the climb and in the cloud layer my plane was starting to accumulate a thin layer of clear ice. I was terrified at this point, I prayed I would just break out of top already. Center asked if I was on top yet and I replied, "no".

Finally at 11,000 feet, I saw light. For only a minute after leveling off at that altitude, my engine started to sputter.

Without thinking and muttering, I chimed to Center and [informed them of my situation]. Unsure of my call for distress, the lead controller asked me to repeat. My engine started again and I was confused, I told him never mind. Big mistake. My engine then proceeded to lose power and from there I did confirm that I [did have an] engine failure. I had no success in restarting the engine.

ARTCC had advised that I had [an airport] to my east for landing and they were to pause all departures and arrivals for me. He then handed me off to Tower Control in which he was giving me vectors for any runway. Luckily, I had a lot of altitude to work with. Tailwinds at the time were strong out of the west so I told him I would like Runway XX.

I carried my speed quicker and realized I would pick up more ice in the descent. As I remember, the controller vectored me for a wide left pattern for the runway until I broke out of the clouds with a 3 mile final. Under stress, I came in high on the glideslope and without thinking used my second notch of flaps. I then came to realize that I was encountering a strong headwind so I took out my flaps. I was going to be low on Runway XX and knew if I was going to continue I would hit the Approach Lighting System (ALS).

At the last second, I veered right in an attempt to land on the taxiway. I touched down in the grass a few feet short of the pavement which sprung me up onto the taxiway. The aircraft then slowed to a complete stop and emergency vehicles moved in. They saw fuel draining out of my fuel vent and said I needed to get away from the plane.

After receiving medical attention, I had reported to the responders that I felt very short of breath and they gave me supplemental oxygen. It took me nearly 24 hours for me to finally recover to breath normally. Although my pulse calmed down, I was still feeling the symptoms of hypoxia. They took me and towed my aircraft to the FBO.

At the time I was very confused on why I lost the engine. I sat there had thought about possible reasons on why it occurred.

I spoke with the owner and another pilot who occasionally does the trips. They told me they suspected icing which blocked the air filter. They also said they were curious to see if the aircraft would start up again. I told him I would try whenever I had the chance in an attempt to find the cause.

After the fuel vent had slowed to a drip, I requested if I could be taken to the aircraft. I was given consent from Airport Rescue and Fire Fighting (ARFF) to start up the plane. With no success, I came to realize that the ferry tank was empty, but the wings were still full. I had operated it the way the owner instructed me to so I was confused. The special airworthiness certificate packet had stated that there is supposed to be instructions on how to operate it provided during flight to the pilot. Of course, I had no luck on finding that. The only instructions I remembered was the 1-2 minute spew the owner gave me.

Lessons Learned:

I feel as the contributing factors were get-there-itis, insufficient flight planning and poor judgment.

There were three critical turning points which occurred that could have been avoided in this flight: hypoxia, icing and fuel starvation. Hypoxia is no joke. What I learned is that it can differentiate depending on the certain conditions, for me I believe the lack of sleep, eating and being at higher altitudes could have caused it. It affected my performance and decision making throughout the flight.

With the icing conditions, I had encountered in climbs and descents, I should learn to watch for weather patterns in unfamiliar regions more closely. The idea of flying a bottom chain aircraft long distances is limiting. No boots, poor performance, no radar, oxygen, etc. It doesn't matter if the aircraft is brand new or however much time you have in the plane, it will still have the same limits in versatility.

With these two factors contributing to the third, fuel starvation. To my own conclusion, I had operated the ferry fuel system insufficiently. The reason why the fuel vent was leaking was because the line that pumps fuel into the left wing pumped 14-15 gallons/hour when I was only burning around 8-9 gallons/hour. What I was supposed to do was switch back and forth between the left wing tank and ferry fuel tank. I ran out of fuel in the ferry tank which led to fuel starvation resulting in engine failure. I had thought it was going to be a self-sustaining system.

Overall, it was a difficult lesson well learned. It's a hard pill to swallow knowing that I had the perfect recipe for disaster. Theoretically, I was not supposed to make it out alive. I was traumatized enough, I vowed to never let this happen to me again. To never accept any sketchy opportunities without proper planning and research. I could have stopped and landed at the closest airport to continue the next day or even call it off. My will to get this flight done and not to disappoint customers out spoke my judgment.

Not all flights go as planned, but we learn that this is aviation.

Delay is always better than a disaster.

I had proper reasoning and so many factors working against me, I should have just discontinued. I was the sole PIC during the flight and no one was there to tell me what to do. The red flags were peer pressure, time commitments, short notice, money, single engine piston over the ocean and lack of team members to fly along with. As you can see here, the risk assessment was already high before the flight was even conducted.

I didn't need the money or flight time. Just breaking enough flight time for ATP, I thought of this as my last hoorah before I went to the airlines. It'd be a fun experience builder. I was wrong. It does not matter what experience level you are as well because it can happen to anyone and I got to see it in a first-hand account. No one told me to do the trip and it could have all been avoided.

With that being said, I am extremely lucky and blessed to be with helpful and caring people that day who saved me.

They executed everything perfectly and I am able to come home to my family for [the holidays]. From that, I am able to build my moral judgment and character on future flights and my career. I feel as I now have the courage whenever I become a Captain somewhere to be confidently decline if ever situated with a difficult problem and it will be valuable down my career. I can take a risk assessment next time I am faced with it.

I will most definitely bring up this case as an example for future aviators in hopes they will never make the same decision I made that day and from that I am gifted to come out unharmed to be able to take the skies again another day.

NOTES:

NO FUEL AND AIRPORT CLOSED
FOR CONSTRUCTION

ASRS, 2014

The trip was my first long distance, multiple fuel stop cross country plan in unfamiliar territory as PIC. When I called Flight Service for a briefing, I was not notified that one of the airports where I intended to land for fuel was closed for maintenance.

I fully fuelled the airplane and departed our home airport. The takeoff was a soft/short field type due to the grass runway length, and my load of two passengers and one bag.

I made the ascent to cruising altitude of 3,500 MSL. When I reached cruising altitude I leaned the mixture according the POH. During the first leg of the flight I was cruising at 3,500 MSL and getting a little push from a tailwind. I was monitoring my ground speed and it was consistent throughout this portion of flight. The first fuel stop was exactly 2 hours into the trip and both fuel gauges indicated that my tanks were more than half full. The next stop was planned to be 90 minutes according to my navigational equipment so I thought I had enough fuel to make the airport with reserve fuel, so I continued without the first fuel stop.

I was conscious of my fuel situation as I continued to monitor the fuel gauges. By the time I had flown well beyond the last available alternative fuel stop before my planned stop, my fuel gauges read one quarter full but were heading toward empty at a faster rate than the first three quarters of the burn. I also noted that I had lost about 10 mph of ground speed for about 10 minutes during this last portion of flight so I considered turning around and going back. I quickly realized that I was midway between the alternative and destination, so turning around into a headwind was not a viable option.

I was getting uncomfortably low on fuel when I announced my approach at 10 miles and the FBO informed me that the airport was closed. I was beginning to plan my descent from 3,500 MSL to pattern altitude. Instead I pulled the throttle back to 1,500 RPM and trimmed the nose up to slow the plane, conserve fuel and buy time. While the airplane gained 500 feet in altitude I made a standard rate turn to the left trying to identify an alternative landing area. I noticed that my fuel gauges were both bouncing off of empty so I knew I had some fuel, but not much. There were three restricted airports within gliding distance but I was unsure of their condition. I asked the FBO whether it was possible to land and was informed that I needed to declare an emergency to do so. I believed that was my best option.

I was five miles from the airport at 4,000 MSL and had slowed to best glide speed. I deployed 30 degrees of flaps and slipped the airplane to lose altitude in a steep descent. The angle of my approach was extreme so just prior to the flare I throttled up and made a safe and smooth landing.

Because the airport was closed I could not depart so we rented a car and continued our journey on wheels.

Lessons Learned:

Poor planning leads to poor performance.

NOTES:

NERVES INCREASED DUE TO NOT BEING FULLY PREPARED

ASRS, 2018

As a student pilot on my second solo cross-country flight, I was preparing to depart ZZZ for ZZZ1. The wind was from 040, so Runway 05 was in use at the time. Looking at the A/FD while parked at the municipal FBO, I deduced that the best way to taxi to Runway 05 was to taxi to Runway 28, then taxi along Runway 28 to the east side of the field, then taxi to the beginning of Runway 05.

After brief confusion about how to taxi to the runway (recent construction at ZZZ has blocked the direct taxi route to the intersection of Runways 05 and 28 seen in the A/FD), I taxied up to the hold line for 10/28, made a radio call announcing my intentions to taxi along Runway 28, looked for traffic along and above said runway, and proceeded to turn left onto Runway 28 and begin taxiing. I did not stop before the intersection of the runways and make a radio call, but continued onwards.

Approximately 50 feet before the intersection, I observed to my left a recently-landed aircraft on Runway 05 approximately 100 yards from the intersection rolling towards me.

Doubting my ability to stop before the intersection, I firewalled the throttle to rapidly cross Runway 05, admitted my error and apologized over the radio, and after a brief stop to gather my nerves, departed and continued my solo cross-country flight.

Lessons Learned:

The problem arose due to my lack of familiarity with the airport and complete inexperience with taxiing along intersecting runways. A contributing factor was that I did not hear a call from the other airplane stating that they were on final, which would have warned me of a landing aircraft.

This trip was my first experience with traveling to a new airport that I had not previously been to with my instructor. Although I thought I had properly prepared for the flight, I obviously was not fully prepared for operating out of the airfield - especially with the construction having altered the taxiways.

I had planned for takeoffs and departures from Runway 10, and had not figured out the return to the departure end of Runway 05 ahead of time when the winds ended up different than expected. Every field that I have flown to before either has parallel taxiways or requires back-taxiing along the departure runway itself. This was my first time ever taxiing along an inactive runway, and I had never crossed a runway intersection when I was not either landing or taking off.

While I am obviously required to stop before crossing any runway while taxiing, I am used to stopping before hold lines - and had never had to deal with the absence of one.

Right before I announced my intention to taxi onto Runway 28, I heard a call from an airplane on a left downwind for Runway 05. I did not hear a call from any aircraft on base or final, which may have warned me of the impending situation. It is possible that a call was made by the other airplane on long final while I was trying to figure out my taxi path, and I simply missed it due to the distraction.

In summary, the cause of this problem was pilot error due to inexperience. The experience gained by this event will hopefully prevent its recurrence. In the meantime, I have grounded myself from flying solo until I can conduct a flight review and another dual cross-country trip with my CFI.

NOTES:

CHAPTER 2

SITUATIONAL AWARENESS

"EVERY PILOT REMEMBERS his first flight. For me, it was in a Cessna 172 at Moody Air Force Base in Valdosta, Georgia, in 1968."

President George W. Bush

ALERT TO THE DANGER

CASA, 2015

It's funny how a chance discussion with another pilot before and after a flight can bring home some important safety lessons. This lesson was about avoiding the hazards associated with flying in the vicinity of non-controlled aerodromes.

I fly out of Tyabb Airport on the beautiful Mornington Peninsula south of Melbourne [Australia]. Recently, when walking to my Cessna 172 to do the pre-flight checks, another pilot stopped me and asked if I could help with the lock on his aircraft door. During our quick discussion he mentioned that he had been ill, and that today was to be his first flight, taking a friend, in quite a while.

I wished him well and continued to my aircraft, casually thinking, 'I hope he flies the plane better than he gets into it', and 'I hope he's OK after not flying for a while'. I also thought about 'must be cleared by a DAME if impairment was for 30 or more days' and 'must not fly as PIC with passengers unless at least three take-offs and landings in previous 90 days'.

After take-off, I noted that we appeared to be the only two aircraft flying at that time. As he had taken off and departed the circuit before I finished my pre-start checks, my radio was not yet on, so I missed his radio calls. I thought that perhaps I should have asked him where he was going to fly that day (situational awareness).

On returning from solo practice in the training area over French Island, Westernport Bay, I made an inbound radio call including my position and altitude. A few seconds later there was an inbound radio call from another pilot giving the same position and altitude as me. I recognised his call sign: it was the pilot I had briefly spoken to before take-off. But there was no mention from him that he had my aircraft in sight.

Lesson one: if you haven't sighted the traffic, say so.

I quickly did some extra scanning in all directions, but could not see him. I thought that we could be very close to each other, and maybe closing.

I instinctively turned on all my remaining outside lights, and after an extra-good scan, turned away from the airport in a gentle left-hand 360 degree turn to get well out of the way.

Lesson two: turn on external lights in vicinity of non-towered aerodromes, and change heading to create relative movement to help detection and avoid collision.

I still could not see him, but then I heard his radio call joining the circuit mid-downwind, so I knew he was now well in front of me and well out of the way. On overflying the airport before descending to circuit height on the dead side and joining crosswind, I heard his base and final radio calls and could easily see him.

Back on the ground we had another brief discussion. He said he first saw me with all my outside lights on turning to the left. He had been well behind me, a little higher and slowly descending.

Lesson three: look before descending!

Lessons Learned:

I thought later that perhaps after his inbound radio call I could have made a radio call asking him if he had me in sight, but recognising that we could be very close and closing, I judged that time was of the essence and so I opted to do what I did ('aviate, navigate, communicate').

It worked and I reckon I did the right thing. I know my inbound call was accurate in terms of position and altitude, but I am not so sure about his.

NOTES:

THOUGHTFUL ANALYSIS OF A
LOSS OF CONTROL SITUATION

ASRS, 2018

This was the day of my first student solo. I had completed an hour of solo flight in the pattern earlier that day after 3 laps in the pattern with my instructor.

On the seventh lap of the second session, I practiced a slip to landing to XX, leveled out at about 10 feet AGL, and believe I caught a wake from a previously departing aircraft, even though I had taken precautions to avoid the affected parts of the runway. I immediately went around.

During the upwind I set cruise RPMs of 2,400, noted the correct airspeed of ~120kts, noted that I was a touch high and pulled some power, called downwind to the tower, was cleared to land, and completed my pre-landing checklist.

I started my setup for descent (pull power from 2,400 RPM to ~1,575) while gradually adding back pressure to increase the nose-up attitude appropriate for level flight with slower speed as the plane as the decelerated, pull carb heat which further drops the power to 1,500.

Put in three rolls down on the trim wheel, wait and watch for airspeed to indicate ∼80 KTS, then add 3 seconds of flaps (∼10 degrees of flaps), verify flaps, push over to nose down to set my descent picture, check correct trim with only fingertip pressure required on the yoke, verify FPM, clear right and start the turn to base. During this process, before pushing the nose over, I noted that when I was still in a "level" to "nose-up" picture, with speed dropping from 90-80 IAS, I was descending already at almost 500 FPM. This was with just over 80 KTS indicated and a slightly nose-high attitude. This confused me a bit because I usually don't see much vertical speed until I purposefully drop the nose after adding flaps.

I then dropped the nose as usual and started a shallow right turn. A few seconds after the stable turn was established at about 20 degrees with the controls neutralized, I felt and saw the plane nose down even more, felt I was falling toward the right door and was "light" in my seat and saw the plane suddenly started increasing its roll to the right. I immediately corrected with left aileron and rudder to level the plane, which took more effort and time than normal, saw the VSI was pointing down (about 1,000 FPM down), checked the IAS (around 80), and started pulling up as I knew I had enough airspeed to do so without stalling.

While pulling up my airspeed decayed to an IAS under 70 KTS and I started to feel some buffeting, which I took as an indication of an accelerated stall. At this point I didn't understand what was going on felt there must be something wrong with the controls related to the left ball I had seen earlier and released back pressure, which again accelerated me downward visually, while not increasing airspeed much.

I was extremely confused. I wondered if that left ball meant I was slipping without intending to, or that some control had "let go" or cable had slipped, or did I have a split flap or ????? And why did pulling up at 70 KTS feel like I was stalling?

I had never been in this situation before.

I had enough indicated airspeed to do typical maneuvers, had tried to level out but felt I was still dropping while nose-up and potentially stalling.

This plane usually stalls at under 45 KTS IAS, but was descending extremely rapidly for the control inputs, and seemed to be accelerating downward with reference to the outside even though my airspeed wasn't keeping pace with the view of the landscape now getting closer by the second. In the flight recorder, my pull up shows a GPS speed of 107 KTS and continued drop of -401 FPM while at +.5 degrees pitch, even though I believe my IAS showed about 80. Again, normally at +.5 degrees pitch, I would have ballooned upwards and slowed down at the same time. At this point I was roughly 300 feet AGL, which put me 250 feet above buildings and obstacles. I was mystified and scared and thought I was going to crash.

I could not figure out what else to do, and was convinced at that moment that there was something wrong with the plane. I radioed tower to [advise them].

I remembered what my instructor had said and what the books said: fly the plane, fly the plane, fly the plane, fly it to the ground. All this time I could hear the tower calling to clear the space airport and keep planes away from the runway.

I then looked for a place to land or crash, feeling there was no way I could make the airfield at these descent rates, continued a shallow turn to the right to line up with a large street, and added full throttle to delay/lessen vertical impact while again pulling up. I believe I radioed the tower again telling them I had lost control and was headed for the street, but I am not sure I remember correctly whether I radioed that or just thought it.

At that very moment, above the power lines, I noticed that my descent had stopped increasing in rate, and even though I was still descending (per recorder over 500 FPM) that I was able to pull the nose up with a more "normal" response.

My descent slowed dramatically more than it had slowed about 20 seconds before when I tried pulling up, and since I was at full power, I was not decreasing IAS dramatically while pulling up.

My IAS looked to be climbing from ~75 to 80. At that point I saw the grass of the airfield to the right between two buildings and thought I would try to put the plane into the grass or some empty spot rather than on top of a busy street, and turned right between the buildings where I could see the grass of the airfield. At this point I was roughly 80 AGL and about 50 feet over the power lines and building roofs, The plane was pitched up at 2.5 degrees, I was now accelerating with full throttle and my last glance at the IAS showed 90 KTS. Usually this configuration is good for ~4-500 FPM of climb but I was still descending at over 200 FPM at 60 feet AGL. I still didn't feel the plane was responding "normally," but could see the "light at the end of the tunnel" as I thought I would at least clear the airfield fence and get into the grass.

As I came over the airport fence, I saw the taxiway was clear to my right, and that [an aircraft] was taxiing toward it from the left, and right at that moment heard the tower call to ask him to stop so I knew they could see me (I think they called "he's going for the taxiway"), although I think the pilot had seen me already because I saw his nose squat and plane stop right as the tower keyed the mike. With the length of the taxiway clear and nobody heading for it I decided to land there instead of the grass. I also noted that as I cleared the fence, the dramatic downward "fall" had stopped and the plane, at this point in ground effect, was behaving close to normal. As I thought to deploy flaps, a final check on the IAS to verify within the white arc showed about 90 KTS. I was in a shallow bank over the taxiway, so pulled power, dropped full flaps, landed ungracefully but uneventfully in the taxiway, rolled to the end to be clear of traffic, and started talking with the tower for instructions.

They had me wait there for a few moments, and during that time I visually manipulated and inspected all the controls from the cockpit because I was sure I had experienced some kind of control failure.

I moved every control and secondary control and could not see anything abnormal.

After a few moments, with tower permission I taxied the plane back to the ramp uneventfully and felt a deep sense of shame and fear. I felt I had failed as a student pilot, let my instructor down, must not have been ready for a solo, had "freaked out," almost harmed myself and others, and caused everybody at the airport inconvenience and potentially harm. I was embarrassed to have decided to fly that second hour, and questioned my own judgment.

Back at the hangar, I shut down, and my flight instructor and I then checked the flight controls and surfaces and found everything normal and operational.

During the weekend I spent hours and hours reviewing the flight recorder data and comparing the 60-second section to other normal laps and descents, and trying things out in the flight simulator and reading in forums and other accident reports, as well as re-reading several books about GA accidents. During that time I had several different hypothesis that could explain what had happened:

1. I had accidentally flipped the flaps lever to the "up" (retract) position after lowering them to 10 degrees, causing the plane to drop quickly during the turn (this 172 has a flap lever with a down position that must be held, a neutral position above that, and another neutral position above that which retracts the flaps).

2. And/or I had rolled the trim wheel up three times instead of down, creating a strong nose-down tendency and strong control pressures which I interpreted as "normal" and didn't fight strongly enough.

3. And/or I had lost proprioception/orientation during VMC and nosed the plane down and entered a dive.

4. And/or I had stalled a wing during my turn to base with incorrect control inputs.

5. And/or I had experienced some kind of downdraft/tailwind/wind shear.

I cannot conclusively rule out any of the above, but felt that I could safely return to flying because no matter which of the above were to blame, I should have done things differently, and indeed will do things differently going forward, and that if I took the right corrective action promptly, I could not only avoid this situation, but do it safely and without any drama or fear.

Lessons Learned:

My personal "learnings" are as follows:

- I will be much more conservative of how much I fly during this learning period, and also the amount of stress I put on myself to learn quickly.
- Even as a new student, I should have trusted my gut and not second-thought my instincts, and created time, altitude, and space to get 100% ahead of the plane before staying in the pattern.
- Although I have learned that the yaw I experienced on climb-out was due to fuel moving to the low wing from a previous extended slip (I re-created this scenario afterwards to verify), I should have kept on the same heading after my climb and taken some time as I didn't understand the change to the flight dynamics. Subsequently I have found that about 3-4 minutes of level flight will re-balance the fuel levels, but I will trust myself to create time and space whenever I find that something doesn't conform to my experience.
- This initial "ball" indication caused me to feel something was amiss, and might have slowed my responses later.

- I should have set a safe altitude and direction to do what troubleshooting was necessary, and should not have dismissed anything I didn't understand. This can be very challenging because as a student, we constantly see things we don't understand, but can't tell which are really "out of normal" and which are just "normal" things we haven't encountered yet.
- When things "feel wrong," immediately abort descent, get to straight and level or a climb if safe and possible, and create time and space to troubleshoot.
- When the right wing dropped, I feel I did the right thing to kick top rudder and ailerons to level and try to pull up. I would do that again, but add full throttle.
- At the point of leveling out after the turn to base I should have also gone to full power, even though I felt I was speeding up, because the IAS didn't show that speed increase. While I already knew and practiced many times increasing power to slow a descent rate, I didn't do this right away because I was "aimed down" and could sense a strong disconnect between my "observed" speed (the scenery speeding up and the nose dropping) and the indicated and felt "plane speed".
- The pattern is extremely dangerous: proximity to other planes, multiple turns, and low altitude AGL means that in ~30-45 seconds you can go from pattern altitude to impact, and one needs to be ready at all times to take immediate corrective action: 20 seconds was way too late, and until I had experienced this myself, and looked at the recordings to note that from the onset of realizing that things were not right to 20 feet AGL was 40 seconds, I did not truly understand how dangerous the pattern is. One also can't "train" for wind shear, or for what it feels like to have an accelerated stall at 400 feet AGL.

- While I had practiced go-arounds, power on and off stalls, and unusual attitudes, I had never felt the combination of sensations that I did at that moment.
- I believe I caught some sort of wind shear, strong downdraft and/or tailwind that while increasing my groundspeed, reduced lift, and caused "level flight" and attack angle with respect to the air I was flying in to be about 10-20 degrees down, so that when I went to about "level" pitch, I exceeded the angle of attack or got very close. By the time I "recovered" 25 seconds later, I was in a powered spiral dive, which I extended onto the taxiway.
- I am grateful that my instructor spent a good deal extra time with me after I could have done my solo and instead continued to do hours of dual instruction, forcing me to do different styles of approaches and maneuvers, endless coordination exercises, slow flight and flight in turbulence. Without that excellent instruction and experience, I would have not been able to keep my bank angle low and consistent during that final turn, and know from the outset of that turn that I would arrive aligned over the pavement even though I was over a fence at 20 feet AGL close to trees, with full power, and doing everything outside of the "normal" pattern descent and landing.

By applying any of the learnings above I could have avoided this incident. Although I learned a lot from this incident, I wish it had never happened. I have flown since, but it will take some time to shake this incident off completely. I want to express my gratitude to the tower personnel, the other pilots and my instructor for their encouragement and support during and after this. I hope to never again write another similar narrative.

NOTES:

NEAR MISS WITH MEAT BOMB

ASRS, 2015

After practicing radio work and 8 Takeoffs and Landings at ZZZ (base airport) I went back to the tie down area to plan a flight to ZZZ1. I checked the weather; winds varied between calm and 100. Using ForeFlight, I selected the procedure "Cross-midfield, Teardrop" for Runway 10. I wrote down the UNICOM and pattern altitude for ZZZ1 (122.8 and 2000 FT respectively).

I departed ZZZ on Runway 13, enroute to ZZZ1. At 3,000 FT MSL, I called ZZZ1 UNICOM to announce that I was 7 miles southeast of the field inbound for Runway 10 and would be crossing mid-field at 3,000 FT. I called UNICOM a 2nd time stating that I was 4 miles southeast of the field, inbound for Runway 10 and would be crossing mid-field at 3,000 FT for a tear-drop into the left downwind for Runway 10. At 3,000 FT I called UNICOM a third time to announce that I was directly south of the field at 3000 FT turning to cross midfield. 4th call to UNICOM: When I was about to cross the airfield I announced that I was crossing midfield at 3,000 FT.

Within seconds of my call a parachute jumper dropped in my view at about the 11 o'clock position and approximately 1,000 feet away. He was wearing a red jumpsuit and using a red and white parachute. We made eye contact. I banked to the right and flew northeast out of the airport vicinity. I called UNICOM for a traffic advisory concerning jumpers in the area. Mr. X, at ZZZ1 FBO, called back and said no jumpers are being reported at that time. I told him one just jumped right in front of me — midfield at 3,000 FT. A 2-minute warning was called out over UNICOM instructing that jumpers were in the area and to not fly over the airport. I stayed northeast of the field at 3,000 FT for quite a while.

I called out to Mr. X to get advice as to whether I should return to ZZZ. He said I could go ahead and land when the area was clear. I called UNICOM specifically asking traffic in the area to state their position. They said they were on Final. I stayed in the northeast area at 3,000 FT.

I called UNICOM again asking traffic to state their position. They said they were on the ground. I proceeded into the downwind for Runway 10 on a 45 and landed without incident.

After tying my plane down and speaking with Mr. X at the FBO about the near-miss I drove over to the Sky Diving School, and spoke with 3 instructors leaving the building. They denied that there had been a near-miss. But, if it had happened it was because my radios were faulty, or I had stepped on the Sky Diving pilot's transmission when he gave the 2 minute warning, or my calls to UNICOM were stepped on. Regardless, the pilot was an airline pilot and with lots of experience.

I went inside to find the owner or manager. [The manager] behind the desk was very helpful and made several calls to find out what happened. She called the owner, he did not speak to me and told [her] that there was not a near-miss, saying that he had been on the radio and heard the 2 minute warning call.

After several calls [she] confirmed that the jumper involved in the near-miss was a new instructor.

She called and talked to him for quite a while. I could only hear her side of the conversation. He told her they had done a Hop N' Pop where they let out one diver out at a low altitude of 5,000 FT before release the other divers at a higher altitude. She directly asked him if he had almost gotten hit by a plane. I got the impression that he said, "No."

After several more questions she relayed to me that he did remember seeing me but I was already on the ground and he was at 200 FT. [The manager] called [the owner] back to tell him what she had learned. [The owner] asked to speak to me. He said there had not been a near-miss and that the 2 minute warning was given and that there was nothing else to discuss. I called the FAA Center and reported the Near-Miss.

Lessons Learned:

What I believe caused the problem:

1. After the incident I reviewed the Airport Directory and it states, "Avoid over flights of airport". I should have gone around the airport, entering the downwind of Runway 10 on a 45.
2. The airport is identified on the Sectional as ZZZ1 but is also referred to as ZZZ1 X. I used both names in my transmission but this could have been confusing to the other pilot. I will confirm with the local FBO the preferred call name to use.
3. I believe that the Skydiving Pilot did not call out the 2 minute warning for the diver/ instructor on the Hop N' Pop.
4. The diver was released 2,000 FT above me and had little time to react.
5. I fly a high wing with limited visibility above me and didn't see the parachute until he was in front of me.

6. I will need to get advice from my instructor on what to do different in the future.

NOTES:

RUNWAY EXCURSION AND CONTACT WITH FENCE

ASRS, 2015

I successfully landed at ZZZ, I had overflown the airport looking for a windsock to determine which runway to use on my landing. Arriving from the south there is no windsock visible. I saw a helicopter taking off from runway 32.

I had not been advised on wind conditions from Unicom, as no one answered, so I decided to land on runway 32 taking into account the direction the helicopter was departing.

After a successful landing on my first try, I refuelled and waited for my friend and his wife to arrive. Upon their arrival and after doing a preflight on the aircraft, checking weight and balance and briefing them on the passenger brief prior to takeoff, we back taxied on runway 32, which I announced on CTAF 122.8.

After departing from runway 32 with a headwind right down runway 32 we departed to the west to do some sightseeing, while talking to Approach and receiving a squawk code for flight following.

5 nautical miles from ZZZ, Approach cleared me for squawking VFR (1200), frequency change was approved and radar service was terminated. Switching back to 122.8, I requested information on the wind but received no response. Seeing the same helicopter departing from runway 32 when we were coming in to look at the windsock, I decided to use runway 32, as the weather was unchanged.

After entering the traffic pattern I decided to do a go around prior to being committed to the runway, due to being high in altitude.

After doing a go around, I had the altitude set up perfectly for a landing on the touchdown zone, halfway down the runway indicated by perpendicular white lines across the runway.

Seconds before the main wheels were to touch down a headwind hit the aircraft (estimated to be 5-8 knots) and floated us down the runway further than expected.

When the wheels finally touched the runway, my airspeed indicated 40-45 KTS. I thought we were too far down the runway with our airspeed too low to do another go around, especially with the buildings in front of the runway. When we contacted the runway I applied full brakes. We ran out of runway, with the propeller striking the fence at the end of runway 32.

The fence suffered minor damage, and the aircraft suffered minor damage to the propeller - a bend in one of the blades and the propeller spinner cone, with dents and chips of paint missing.

Lessons Learned:

The windsock cannot be viewed when arriving from the south or west, as the windsock is on top of the building. The weather conditions had not changed from the first successful landing to the landing that ended in a propeller strike, so I had no reason to anticipate gusty wind conditions. I was not advised of current weather conditions at the airport from Unicom.

NOTES:

CONFUSED AND DISORIENTED AFTER TAKEOFF

ASRS, 2011

On departure, the initial climb was pretty smooth, but winds were from the southwest with gusts to 20 knots. I started my turn to the north at about 400 feet AGL, and about then was hit with a burst of turbulence that really rocked the plane. The TAWS unit called out "Obstacle", then "Sink Rate, Pull Up". While recovering from this and re-establishing the climb, I continued my turn through the assigned 350 degree heading to about 60 degrees, toward the incoming aircraft on approach.

During the turbulence, I had tried to flip-flop the radio from tower to departure, but the bumpy ride made me brush my finger against the wrong part of the GTN 650 touch screen, leaving the COM radio on the wrong frequency. While turning, I was re-tuning the radio, and when I got it to the correct frequency I immediately heard the departure controller instructing me to turn back to the 350 degree heading. I turned and climbed and followed the rest of the departure instructions correctly. I was instructed to call ATC on landing, since there was a possible loss of separation.

Partly due to the turbulence and recovery, and partly due to confusion, once I had continued the turn to far toward the east, I misinterpreted the CDI guidance and would have continued the turn. I had turned the ZZZ VOR into the NAV2 radio, which meant that the needle was "reverse sensing". Following the needle at this point was leading me the wrong direction.

Lessons Learned:

I could have avoided some of the confusion if I had programmed the GTN 650 better. I had set it into OBS mode with the 286 radial off of ZZZ VOR, so that it was showing the same guidance as the NAV2 radio. If I had entered it as ZZZ VOR to ZZZZZ Intersection, then the map representation would have been more helpful.

Before takeoff, I had briefed the departure, but had not actually pulled up the enroute chart and drawn in the route, which I would have normally done if it were IMC. I had a casual attitude about the departure procedure, thinking of it as an obstacle departure procedure that wasn't that important since it was VMC. In reality, it's more like a SID, to keep aircraft away from the approach path, but without the graphical representation. When I spoke with the departure controller, he said that they had a lot of problems with pilots not following the Departure Procedure. Perhaps this would be improved if it were published as a SID.

NOTES:

AN UNSAFE DEPARTURE

ASRS, 2015

Narrative: 1

The John C. Tune airport (JWN) in Nashville, TN recently completed a runway renovation project that increased the total runway length of the airport's only runway, 02/20. While the runway has reopened, the construction surrounding the airport remains, and the main parallel taxiway remains mostly closed.

Only one runway exit at taxiway A-1 remains open, and it is situated at the approach end of runway 2. This requires aircraft that are departing on runway 20 or landing on runway 2 to back taxi along the runway, and other aircraft to hold short of taxiway A-1 so as to provide space for aircraft exiting the runway.

Other pertinent information relevant to this discussion is that the Nashville Approach Clearance Delivery frequency on 124.55 for use on the ground at John Tune is currently out of service.

There are multiple NOTAMS about the construction at the John Tune airport describing all of this, and more.

However, despite this we have had a number of near collisions and runway incursions since the airport reopened. I will describe my most recent experience below.

I was giving instruction to a trainee in the pattern of the John C. Tune airport. My student and I were near the end of our flight and flying a Cessna 172.

The traffic pattern was empty, and no incoming airplanes had called on the CTAF that they were inbound. My student performed a touch-and-go on runway 20 and we were on the departure leg for runway 20 when we heard the following. [Question was asked by another GA pilot in regard to the Clearance Delivery frequency. One aircraft announced his position in the pattern and one aircraft announced that he was performing a back taxi on the runway for departure.]

A minute or so later, the Cessna back taxiing for departure on runway 20 reaches the departure end of runway 20 and turns around preparing to depart. My student turned about a 1.5 mile final for runway 20. About 30 seconds later we hear: "[Aircraft] on departure!"

I look up and found an aircraft flying approximately 300 feet above the Cessna 172 at the approach end of runway 20, heading opposite our direction and offset slightly to our left. He had taken off on runway 2 despite knowing there was one airplane still on the runway, departing from the opposite end, and another (us) on final approach for the opposite runway 20.

My student and I veered right and initiated a go around and passed abeam the Mooney by approximately 500 feet at the closest point.

I called on the radio, "[Aircraft make-model], are you still on the John Tune frequency?" I received no reply.

At that point, my student and I offset from the runway and allowed the other Cessna to depart, then we initiated a normal right pattern and full-stop landing on runway 20.

The aircraft in question, endangered the lives of at least 5 people (including his own) in a reckless and intentional manner. He was clearly aware there were two conflicting airplanes on or near runway 20, and he chose to depart runway 2 opposite that traffic even while one of the airplanes was still sitting on the opposite end of the runway.

Further, there is a substantial terrain rise in the middle of the runway preventing an airplane at runway 2 from seeing the end of runway 20. Thus, there is no way he could know that the Cessna had not yet begun its takeoff roll.

Narrative: 2

John C. Tune Airport (JWN) has recently undergone extensive airport, runway, and taxiway reconstruction and has just recently reopened. It currently has several operational restrictions. Taxiway A1 at the south end of the airport is the only open taxiway. This only allows immediate access to runway 2 for departure. The only way to depart runway 20 is to taxi north up the full length of the runway and turn around on the runway.

As the applicant prepared to announce that we would be taking the runway for back-taxi and departure on runway 20, a [pilot] asked local traffic if the remote clearance delivery frequency 124.55 was working, since he could not receive his IFR clearance. The flight instructor in the Cessna 172 operating in the traffic pattern for runway 20, explained that the clearance delivery frequency was not working at that time, and that this is explained in current airport NOTAMs. The 172 continued to report each leg in the traffic pattern.

Per recommended protocol, my student applicant made all necessary radio calls to notify other local traffic that we were "back-taxiing" down the full length of the runway for departure on runway 20. This call was acknowledged by the flight instructor in 172, who was then on right base leg for runway 20.

We then heard the [GA pilot] call that he was taxiing to the runway. We subsequently heard him call that he would hold short of the runway. We assumed that he was waiting for us and the 172 to vacate before taking the runway for back-taxi and departure on 20 himself.

The applicant and I continued our taxi down the runway. As we turned around, we saw the [other aircraft] on departure from runway 2, right above our position on the runway, not more than 100 feet AGL. I called to the 172 that the [other aircraft] had actually taken off and was heading toward him. The 172, on final at that point, called that he was going around. When challenged on the radio, the [departing] pilot made no response.

Lessons Learned:

Narrative: 1

The safety lesson I can draw from this is to never assume that your fellow pilots are merely ignorant. Rather, adopt the defensive assumption that they are actively trying to kill you. Luck was the only factor preventing an otherwise easily avoided tragedy brought on by one pilot's impatience.

Callback Comment:

Reporter indicated that this is a very busy non-towered airport and he feels that it should have a tower. He described several other ground conflicts as well as near-mid-air collisions while operating in the traffic pattern. He added that the taxiway has recently reopened which may reduce the ground conflicts, but he hopes that a tower will be considered.

NOTES:

CHAPTER 3

COMPLACENCY & FATIGUE

"Suddenly with no warning the engine stopped. From the startled look on the instructor's face I knew this was no test."

172 student pilot

A FEW HOME TRUTHS

CASA, 2014

I was 40 years old before I could achieve a long-time ambition to fly. Over the next 20 years as a PPL holder I managed a few hundred hours on Cessnas and Pipers, gaining a night VMC rating and a formation flying endorsement. Now nearing 80 years old, and no longer flying, I can only look back on my excellent formal training and on the informal advice from more experienced pilots that enabled me to do this without even scratching an aircraft or scaring a passenger.

You can learn a lot about safety by listening to hangar talk. What do you do on a 'touch and go' when the full flaps refuse to retract and the end of the short strip is fast approaching? Recycle the flap settings – that sometimes works. It did for me. What happens on a cold starry night at 5,000 feet, miles from anywhere, when the previously smoothly purring single engine begins to cough and splutter? Apply full carb heat and hope any ice is melted quickly. Again, that worked for me.

Acting as check pilot during club competitions in a venerable Cessna 150, what is the correct protocol when the ex-RAAF PIC with thousands of hours on the most sophisticated aircraft, but few on the Cessna, is about to 'go round' with full flap extended? Say 'flaps' very firmly and audibly. And we cleared the trees bordering the country strip with room to spare.

Sometimes, however, a problem arises which you have not heard discussed. One occurred when, as a student, I was completing my final five-hour navigation exercise to gain an unrestricted licence.

The instructor arrived at the field late, but I had prepared well in advance and we took off soon after.

Three incidents occurred during the flight, none of which I really understood until several days later.

I had planned for BO50 but my instructor told me to climb to 9500 feet, saying he would do the necessary communication with ATC. I was happy to 'aviate' and' navigate', leaving the 'communicate' part to him. Soon after reaching the new level I heard a mildly reprimanding ATC on the radio telling us that we were on the incorrect frequency, and should change to the one he was giving us. Embarrassing, but not really my problem. I thought the instructor was using the incident to impress upon me the importance of correct communication. He definitely succeeded.

Arriving over a country airport where a landing was planned I was meticulous in letting down to circuit height on the 'dead' side, and accurately flying the crosswind and downwind legs. I was really anxious to impress this instructor. Imagine my horror when on turning base to finals I was asked, 'do you intend to land downwind?' The windsock clearly showed I was landing into wind. I pointed out this fact to the instructor who then agreed with me and we landed uneventfully. Once again I assumed this was part of the test I was undergoing to become an unrestricted pilot.

Fuel checks on the ground showed we had sufficient fuel for the flight home. Back in the air I was given an unexpected diversion to an unknown locality.

I thought I handled the diversion well. Just 15 minutes out from home base I was feeling comfortable with my day's performance. True, the instructor had not said much on the flight but we were not there to chat; my job was to convince him that I flew well enough for my licence restriction to be lifted. Suddenly with no warning the engine stopped. From the startled look on the instructor's face I knew this was no test.

It was the only time before or since that I have had an engine quit on me in flight. The silence is awesome. In less time than it takes to tell, I recognised the cause of the engine failure and fixed the problem by reaching down and changing fuel selection from left to right tank on the console of the Cessna 172. The engine immediately started. I had run the left tank dry.

Before that day I had always flown with fuel selection on both, ignoring the left/right switches. On this flight the instructor overrode my choice, saying that tanks should be alternated each 30 minutes for a more balanced flight. He took it upon himself to make the change, doing so several times – and with no real choice I was not going to argue with him. But somehow in the final stages of this flight he forgot to make the switch. The left tank was exhausted. No harm was done, as the other tank held adequate fuel. I completed the day's exercise successfully.

A few days later I found out why my instructor, normally really sharp with his instruction, had been so far off his game as to make three errors with a student, one of which (at least) could have been serious and all of which were embarrassing and unnecessary.

That morning, before he set off for the training aerodrome, he and wife had argued seriously enough for the D-word to be used. He had spent the day in a highly emotional state of mind.

Sitting beside me for five hours with little to do but chew over his worries he became even more preoccupied with his domestic problems and less aware of what he was doing.

Lessons Learned:

The safety lesson I learned that day has not been forgotten. Flying demands total concentration. Emotional worries and personal concerns must not be taken into the air. And, most definitely, there must be no fight with the wife before flight.

NOTES:

MISSING STARBOARD FUEL CAP

ASRS, 2017

I first arrived at the hangar at about XA00, intending to go out on a flight specifically working on cross-country navigation techniques. I performed a preflight inspection the aircraft, and saw that I had been the last person to fly the aircraft which I verified by checking the Hobbs and Tachometer meters.

Upon receiving the weather briefing for my planned route of flight, I did not quite like the presence of a SIGMET Zulu over nearly the entire flight path, considering it would be VFR over the top for the first half at that time (another thing I much prefer to avoid); beyond that, I also decided that I hadn't gotten enough rest the night prior, so should either not make the flight at all or remedy the situation beforehand.

I secured the aircraft and the hangar, and went home to get a little bit of work done and rest if possible. I returned to the airport, rested, at approximately XF30, and performed only a cursory inspection of the aircraft and systems before turning the engine, since I had inspected it in the morning. This was clearly a big mistake.

I had noticed a few other abnormalities, such as the hangar lock being unlatched, though I am on the OCD side of things, particularly when it comes to locks. I generally also set the lock's combination to 0000 when locking it, and this was not the condition of the lock upon my return. At the time, I noted it was unusual, but saw nothing obvious with the airplane, and so did not think much else of it. I am not saying this to accuse anyone of anything; I believe that during my first, morning inspection of the aircraft, I was not as thorough as I am usually known to be, and attribute this to fatigue.

In flight, I noticed abnormal readings on the fuel tank gauges approximately 30 minutes into the flight; namely, only the left fuel tank's gauge was bouncing around, and the right tank's gauge was stable at around the 75% capacity mark.

I attempted to "shake" the plane around to loosen the fuel gauge floats with no success. As the flight continued, I noticed a slightly increased rolling tendency, requiring constant correction; I then made the decision to perform a precautionary landing at the nearest airport with maintenance and fuel services. I chose ZZZ airport based on its available services, proximity to me at the time, and moderate level of current pilot activity. I landed safely, taxied to the FBO, and examined the aircraft. I found the right wing fuel tank cap was missing. Fortunately, I was able to source a spare at the airport and put a new gasket on it before filling up the tanks to full. I then performed a thorough preflight inspection on the aircraft, and cautiously continued with my flight plan. The rest of the flight was without incident.

Lessons Learned:

I have several takeaways from this series of events:

First and foremost, a complete and thorough inspection shall be performed before every sortie and after every landing, regardless of whether or not the aircraft has been inspected or flown earlier in the day.

Second, any abnormalities with the aircraft or facilities shall again result in a complete thorough inspection of the aircraft.

Third, this is not my job; thus, I am under no obligations of any sort to fly while not well rested, and moving forward, shall cancel any planned or scheduled flights if I am not absolutely at 100%, in the future.

NOTES:

CHAPTER 4

HUMAN FACTORS, & DECISION MAKING

"There are a large number (65) of fuel exhaustion accidents. This suggests improper flight planning or poor in-flight decisions in many cases."

Article - Aviation Consumer
  Regarding accidents over a five-year period

REALLY UNABLE TO REMAIN CLEAR OF THE CLOUDS TODAY

ASRS, 2018

Narrative: 1

I agreed to serve as safety pilot for a colleague in my flying club while he flew practice approaches. We planned to land and then switch seats for him to act as my safety pilot. We agreed before departure that I would serve as PIC for his flight. For my flight I filed IFR because of widespread cloud cover in our area that included forecasts of clouds down to 1,900 feet in places where we would need to be at 3,000 feet to properly practice approaches. He and I both have extensive experience flying IFR in C172s.

When I asked where he planned to fly I asked if he had filed IFR, which I assumed he had because it would be necessary. He said he was going "to remain clear of the clouds today," which struck me as quite unlikely to be feasible. My thought at the time was that he either didn't want to deal with the bother of filing or he did not want his first flight in a new plane to be in the clouds. I told him that didn't seem likely and he said he'd take off and see how it looked up there.

The weather directly over our home airport was VFR but it seemed that the ceilings were only around 2,000 feet and there were lower clouds in the direction of our flight. He insisted that it would be fine and I did not press him on the issue since we had flown together many times and I haven't previously had reason to be concerned about his judgment. I assumed that if the clouds were lower than expected he'd jump on an IFR plan and do the approaches in and out of the clouds. The ceilings would still give us 1,000 feet on breaking out, which seemed like plenty of safety cushion.

Once we departed and turned on course it was clear to me within the first minute that we would not be able to fly to EMI and then to 2W2 VFR at 3,000 feet as hoped. I pointed this out, and he said he was "working on it."

He leveled off around 2,200 feet and after giving him a minute or two I told him I was not comfortable with the situation and suggested that he ask for an IFR clearance. We were approaching 500 feet from the clouds above and he didn't seem to be taking the distance requirement seriously despite me pointing this out.

He went to put his foggles on and I told him not to because we were at risk of going into cloud and we needed to change our plan.

A minute or two later he had been forced by the descending ceiling to fly lower to remain clear of the clouds. At this point I estimate that we were within 100 feet of the clouds. We had a passenger in the back so I put the intercom on "crew" and told the flying pilot that it was just me and him on the intercom now, and that I was very uncomfortable with how close we were to the clouds. I pointed out that there was a tower 300 feet below us, to our two-o'clock, and I noted that we could not continue for more than another minute without flying into a cloud that was straight ahead of us.

He asked for more time to consider his options and was intensely focused on his iPad, probably checking the weather at various airports. He was not looking much outside of the aircraft.

I don't know why he was so hesitant to ask for an IFR clearance but I felt that the safety of the flight was in question, in addition to violating the FARs we were about to fly into a cloud deck in an area that getting hilly and had towers.

Given that he and I had flown together multiple times before and never had any serious problems I was confused about why this was all happening, but I was certain that I was not going to let fear of speaking up lead to inadvertent flight into IMC lead to a loss of control or CFIT crash. I told him clearly that if he got any closer to the wall of clouds directly ahead I was going to [advise ATC], and take control of the plane.

At that point he turned left by about 90 degrees to avoid those clouds and he was trying to stay in VMC. There was some VMC straight and to the left but we had just left the SFRA, were still within 2 miles of its lateral boundaries, and our new heading was putting at risk of crossing it without a clearance.

He then called ATC and said he needed an IFR clearance due to clouds. At this point we were probably around 1,600 or 1,700 feet. ATC quickly gave us climbing instructions, we flew into the clouds, and were vectored for an approach at FDK. He flew that approach just fine and landed safely.

We took a break on the ground for a few minutes and then I flew us home on an IFR flight plan in IMC for the first part of the flight.

When we landed at our home airport he said to me that he was glad that we got that IFR clearance because it was, "the right thing to do." I did not want to have a conversation about it in front of our passenger so we did not discuss the incident further.

When we do discuss it I plan to ask him what he was thinking throughout the process: Why didn't he file IFR at first? Why was he so hesitant to ask for the clearance once it was clear we would need it? Why would he think it was OK to bust the cloud minimum and put us seconds away from flying into clouds less than 2,000 feet from the ground?

Narrative: 2

This was to be a flight to practice IFR approaches at DMW and 2W2. I was the pilot flying. On board was a qualified safety pilot from my flying club. Checking the weather at those airports showed them to be MVFR and FDK was VFR at the time of the flight. I did not file an IFR flight plan for this flight as I was hoping to fly them more quickly than would be the case if flying on an IFR flight plan. Although the ceilings were lower than desired, I made the decision to depart and see what it was like.

It didn't take long after takeoff to see that the clouds were pretty low. As I continued, the clouds started forcing me lower to remain clear of the clouds. During this time I'm sure I came closer than 500 feet below the clouds.

My safety pilot was pointing out to me that this is not a good situation. We are flying too close to the clouds, too close to the ground, were close to penetrating the clouds and need to do something. My response to his request was I'm working on it. We were now out of the DC SFRA and I turned about 90 degrees left towards FDK where the weather appeared better and started fiddling with my iPad for weather at airports near us. My safety pilot insisted we need to get out of this situation now. I then called Potomac Approach and asked for an IFR clearance to FDK. I was given the clearance and ask to climb. This put us in the clouds and I was given vectors for an approach to FDK. After a few minutes, we emerged into VMC and flew a visual approach into FDK.

Lessons Learned:

Narrative: 1

In terms of what caused the incident, I speculate that strong familiarity with the local area may have played an important part of his willingness to fly IMC without a clearance. Both of us have flown these same approaches dozens of times and know the area well.

He may also not have been instrument current, though I am pretty sure he mentioned otherwise.

I spend quite a substantial amount of time reviewing accident reports, reading aviation safety journals, and participating in online scenario reviews. All of my alarm bells were going off and it seemed bizarre to me that he was seemingly so willing to just continue as though there was nothing wrong. Complacency seems to have been a factor but there may have been other things going on his life that I was/am unaware of.

In considering what I should have done differently, I should have asked him before the flight if he was IFR current and what was his backup plan if he could not navigate around the clouds to remain safe and legal.

Narrative: 2

Although I knew the weather was marginal, I made the poor decision to take off VFR. Additional, as we flew along and conditions were becoming worse, I still was of a mindset to continue VFR. I did not plan to scud run or fly VFR into VMC conditions but I ended up scud running and nearly entered the clouds.

I can now understand how easy a mindset can lead a pilot to scud run and potentially fly VFR into IMC. I have learned from this episode and will now file an IFR flight plan before leaving the ground with marginally conditions or not leave the ground at all.

NOTES:

THE PASSENGER TRAP

CASA, 2020
Greg Ackman

It was a lovely day for flying and my two passengers were a husband and wife who owned a business that sold my products.

I was in the city visiting their shop when I mentioned that I recently gained my PPL - they were both very keen to go flying with me. Since I hadn't done a lot of flying recently and being in a different city from my home base, I agreed to take them for a local flight on the following Sunday. As I was still a newbie, I was a bit nervous about renting from the main secondary airport with busy weekend traffic and demanding tower controllers. Luckily, there was another small airfield about 20 nm east with a local flying club and a C172 for hire.

I made an appointment for the Saturday afternoon and did my check ride and local area familiarisation flight in less than one hour. I was well pleased with my check flight at the lovely grassy airfield and, with the help of the local CFI, I planned a one-hour flight the next day to take in the local sights.

On Sunday my booking was for 3 pm which gave me almost 2.5 hours until last light, plenty of time to do the trip. We arrived at 2.30 but were told the aircraft had a flat tyre and the club members were searching for a spare tube. By the time the aircraft was serviceable, it was 4 pm when we taxied out and headed south on the first leg.

The flight was pure magic as we tooled along with the puffy clouds. At 4.30 pm I did a 180-degree turn onto the reciprocal track and started heading back to the grassy field with an ETA of 5.05 pm. However, at about 4.50 pm as we were near the secondary airport, the female passenger expressed a desire for a comfort stop. I advised her it would only be 15 minutes until we landed but she replied the coffee that was consumed during our delay wouldn't wait that long!

I decided it was best to land and called downwind; we were cleared immediately for a landing. At 5.05 pm we again taxied out for the short flight east. As we were number three to depart, I began to get nervous about last light. After 10 minutes we were cleared to line up. The tower controller asked if I was night rated. This caught me by surprise and I answered 'yes' and he immediately cleared me to depart with a right turn to the east. On lifting off I noticed the sun was gone—I turned towards the twilight ahead and the approaching darkness along my track.

I realised later I should have just rejoined the circuit and landed immediately. I foolishly decided to press on to my destination only 10 minutes away so as not to cause perceived embarrassment and inconvenience to myself and the passengers.

We arrived in the circuit area above a dark airfield where I could just make out the buildings and runway. I quickly joined downwind but by the time I was on final, the runway way just a hazy blur. I commenced the flare but, looking at the horizon, found I couldn't see the runway and was descending into a black void. I increased power, pitched up and began to climb out.

When I was at about 500 feet, the radio crackled to life—the club CFI was asking if I was flying their Cessna. I quickly responded and he told me to orbit while they organised lights. Within a couple of minutes, I could see lights moving in the dark. By this time my passengers worked out what was happening and they were freaking out, adding to my stress.

However, there were soon multiple headlight beams aimed down the runway and flashing turn indicators showing the threshold. The approach and landing were uneventful although it did take a while to find the clubhouse in the dark and taxi in. To say the CFI was upset would be an understatement! I was also upset that the aircraft was supposed to be night VFR but had no serviceable instrument, landing lights or a working ADF. The net result was that I paid a fine of a case of beer and the club agreed to fix the aircraft's lighting systems.

Lessons Learned:

I learnt some real lessons that day:

- Don't depart an airfield before last light and fly to another airfield without lights at the destination.
- Make sure before flying, the night VFR aircraft is in fact serviceable for night operations.
- Always contact the aircraft operator if you deviate from the planned flight.
- If you take-off and don't like what's ahead, go back and land immediately.
- Don't ever risk the lives of your passengers for the sake of inconvenience.
- Make sure the passengers have comfort breaks before they fly.

I scared myself silly and my passengers were understandably very upset and, only through the grace of God and the fast and clear action by the club CFI, did my flight have a happy ending.

NOTES:

FLYING THROUGH THE FINAL APPROACH

CASA, 2014

My student and I were inbound to ZZZ during her training so she was under foggles. We asked approach for the Localizer approach to the left runway but they said unable due to multiple arrivals and told us to remain visual.

We loaded the approach anyway for guidance and I told her if we could fly over the FAF then she could log it. Tower put us on a heading vector for left base which had us set up 90 degrees from the FAF with the nose pointed barely north of it. We were cleared to land and told not to overfly final. Autopilot was on and I told my student to leave it in heading mode so we could control our intercept angle.

I made visual contact with the jet airliner on final for the right runway, they were to the right of us while we were still on base. They were close but not to the degree that it alarmed me. I think my sight pictured matched what I assumed was about to be a turn to final.

With my eyes outside, I didn't realize my student was waiting for the localizer to come alive to start the turn toward the runway.

So when it did start to move we blew through it quickly due to the 90 degree intercept angle. Since we were making that turn with autopilot on we were turning at standard rate and about two-seconds later were dangerously close to the final for the right runway.

I lost visual on the jet as we started turning. All at the same time Tower started yelling and my student cut autopilot off and put us in a steep bank to get us back on final for the left runway. I think she saw the jet through her foggles out her window on the right. We heard the jet go missed, I think he said something like "they were just a little too close for comfort." I told her to go visual and she landed.

Lessons Learned:

I learned a lot from this. I started to feel sick earlier in the day and my energy level deteriorated rather suddenly before we flew. I had felt foggy and disoriented since leaving work.

I could have paid better attention to what was going on inside the cockpit rather than fixating on the jet once I had identified it's location.

Sickness caused processing in my head to slow. I am certain I would not have flown if I was going for a joy flight solo, but having work to do and a students' checkride to prepare for was a massive external pressure that I could not brush off.

I believe having autopilot on made my student subconsciously complacent and forgetful that we had not activated the NAV and APR modes on the G1000. And I don't believe traffic alerts work quite the same in the G1000 when an approach is activated.

I'm usually overly careful with parallel approaches as I'm based at this airport and have been in this situation many times. Today my reaction time wasn't what it normally is. I'm grateful the pilots of the airliner had been paying attention as we could have caused something more serious.

NOTES:

GET-HOME-ITIS NEARLY STRIKES

CHIRP, 2020

I took a passenger from [home airfield] to [Airport]. It's a flight which is about 30 minutes in duration in a C172. I had the club's plane booked from 1400 - 1600.

The plan was: take off at 1415, on the ground at [Airport] by 1445, quick coffee, back in the air by 1515, on the ground at [home airfield] by 1540 (the wind was northerly so the flight back would have been quicker). The departure from [home airfield] was slightly delayed because I took my time with the pre-flight check, and the passenger was very curious, asking me to explain my actions to him in great detail. But the flight itself was uneventful, and we landed at about 1455.

We walked out through security, hoping to get a quick burger and fly back. But by the time the officer at the security desk arranged for the payment of the landing fee, all we had time for was to go outside, get some fresh air and walk straight back in.

We were ground side (as opposed to airside) for maybe five to seven minutes, tops. This is when the trouble began.

I knew I had to be on the ground at [home airfield] by 1600. Two reasons: the plane was booked by somebody else from 1600 to 1800 for some night training; and sunset was at 1625. I'm not night-rated so, by law, the latest I could fly was 1655 - but I thought that would be unwise.

As we walked up to the security desk, the officer asked for my licence and photo ID. I'd left my licence on the plane, so it took a while to work through that issue, but it was quickly resolved. He then asked for my passenger's photo ID. This requirement for a photo ID to go through the airport gate as a passenger is not in the flight guides for that particular airport, and I had certainly never encountered this before in all my flying. "The only thing I have on me is my driving licence," my passenger said. "Oh, that's more than enough," answered the security man, then looked at the document - and his expression suddenly became very stern. "Do you know, Sir, that it's out of date? I'm afraid I can't let you through," he said.

My options at this stage were: to either leave the passenger where we were, expecting him to make his own way back to our field where his car was parked (two trains and a bus ride), or to beg and nag. I chose the latter option. The begging and nagging, and the resulting frantic calls from security to management and back to security - took quite a long time. I even had to call the Tower and ask them for help, but there wasn't much they could do. "I'm only following procedures, Sir," was all the officer was prepared to say.

I called the club to warn them I was running late and to apologize to the pilot who had the next booking. Stress was beginning to pile up. By the time the issue was resolved ("You can go, but we'll have to escort you to the plane and watch you leave"), it was 1555. As I said, the sunset was 1625, so I was, by now, cutting it fine.

I rushed through pre-take off checks ("nothing's fallen off, we've got enough fuel and oil, all surfaces move").

I rushed through the departure (rolling take-off, steep turn on course immediately after noise abatement).

I rushed through everything imaginable, flying the poor C172 at 120 knots all the way.

I was so stressed and goal-oriented that I actually had a brain-freeze when I needed to adjust course to whatever heading I needed. For a few moments I just sat there and tried to figure out whether I should be turning left or right!

Lessons Learned:

In hindsight, I broke a number of rules which I vouched never to break: no get-home-it is; always preflight the aeroplane properly; and do not fly if stressed. By the time we got back it was still OK in terms of light, and I was still very, very legal, with at least 20 minutes to spare. But ATC at my field threw me another curveball and asked for an approach which would be "as tight as you can, please". Which was fine, but looking back at the video my passenger shot, I can see I was lower than I should have been in an ideal world, and landed somewhat to the left of the centreline. I would probably rate that approach as a 7 out of 10. This is not normally my style, - more signs of stress and task saturation? Lessons learned: get pax to carry a valid photo ID at all times, stop and think, learn to breathe out and disconnect from the stress before taking off.

CHIRP Comment:

This report contains many good flight safety lessons and provides a timely reminder about how external influences can mount up to cause serious distractions and unwanted pressure to complete tasks to the detriment of safety. Most pilots set personal rules and boundaries to avoid operating beyond their personal comfort zones – and there are many temptations for pilots to break their own rules on occasion.

This was a good example of how situations can build up to pressurise pilots beyond the point of prudence, and how difficult it can be to call a halt to things as you are 'nibbled to death by ducks'.

It's easy to say in hindsight but, at some point when beset by seemingly conflicting priorities, pressures and obstacles, pilots need to have the moral courage to stand back and look at the bigger picture to assess whether what they are trying to achieve and their continued course of action is really sensible.

<u>NOTES:</u>

EMERGENCY LANDING

ASRS, 2014

I visually checked the fuel level before this flight. It appeared full, on both sides. I had asked the lineman, a few days earlier, to top the fuel tanks and he agreed to. While the fuel was not touching the fuel caps, I guessed that he had left "room" for expansion, to avoid it running onto the hangar floor.

I flew for approximately three hours, at which point the aircraft lost power. It should have only burned approximately 27 gallons in three hours. It either burned more than 9 gallons/hour or it was not as full as it appeared, because the usable fuel quantity for this aircraft is 38 gallons. The right gauge even indicated 1/4 full.

So, at 3,500 FT MSL, when the aircraft lost power, I immediately turned toward the closest airport, gliding as far as possible. I banked back and forth, checked fuel settings, changed tanks, checked mixture, etc. It then regained power for approximately 30 seconds, then completely quit.

I thought we might make it to the airport, but when it was clear that that wouldn't be possible, I selected a field that looked level, without trees.

I ended up making a smooth landing, but in a wheat field. No damage occurred to the aircraft and thankfully, no one was injured.

While fuel is always the responsibility of the P.I.C., the reality is the lineman failed to top it off. It was evidently approximately 10 gallons less than full, but the exact amount is impossible to ascertain with a visual inspection.

Lessons Learned:

The best lesson here is that if the fuel is not touching the fuel caps, it is imperative to use a fuel stick to get an accurate measurement of the fuel level.

It is impossible to know how much fuel is in the tanks otherwise. I will always use a fuel stick in the future if the fuel is not touching the caps.

<u>NOTES:</u>

DECREASING ENGINE POWER

ASRS, 2017

I did the preflight as usual and nothing stood out of the ordinary. It had 7.5 QT of oil and 1/2 tank of fuel in each tank. Slight tire wear on the left main wheel with no chord showing.

Engine start was smooth with two primes. Both oil pressure and temp remained in green and the battery was charging fine. During taxiing to the run up engine was running fine at 1000 RPM. All engine gauges were in green.

Engine run up started with auxiliary fuel pump on for a second just to see the rise in fuel flow. Throttle was advanced to 1800 RPM for the mag check.

Before starting the mag check the engine seemed to be rough running. So throttle was advanced to 2100 RPM and the leaned the mixture and kept it running for 30 seconds. Then brought back the throttle to 1800 RPM for the mag check with the mixture turned rich about 2 turns in but completely rich. The left and right mag drop were within limitations. All engine gauges were green. Throttle idle check was within limits.

After, we went for pattern work and completed 3 patterns to a full stop taxi back with no engine problem.

On the 4th pattern, a soft field take off configuration was chosen, with flaps set 10 degrees. As we were cleared for takeoff, mixture was put to full rich, and throttle advanced to full. After main wheels came off of runway, airplane was flown in ground effect until climb speed, at which point the engine was noticed to be 'pulsing', lightly at first but getting rapidly worse, a cross check of engine gauges indicated all were in the green, and VSI was indicating a no-climb situation at 250 feet AGL. The power was noticeably decreased to the point, with the throttle still at full power setting. As a result, the attitude was pitch up in an attempt to climb but this did no good.

The flight controls were transferred to the CFI at this point, and a right turn to attempt a landing on the opposite, adjacent runway was initiated.

Instructor informed tower that engine was running rough and needed to immediately return for landing on the opposite runway. Tower cleared to land on 30R. The turn was steepened due to power lines observed near to the aircraft and the stall horn sounded, indicating the low airspeed, seen around 55 KTS by both the student and the instructor.

After aligning on 30L, [another] aircraft was seen by the CFI aborting its takeoff roll and the CFI sidestepped to Runway 30R. The aircraft touched down midfield on its right main landing gear, followed by left and then nose gears, still with 10-degrees of flaps from the soft field configuration takeoff. The aircraft on a short final was instructed by tower to go around. Took taxiway C under own power, with roughness observed while taxiing.

ATC asked if assistance was required, which declined. While taxiing at 1500 RPM, not enough momentum was being provided as at 1000 RPM, but was still sufficient to return to [the] ramp.

After returning to the main ramp, a brief run-up was preformed, with slight roughness noted at around 2100 RPM. Aircraft was then shut down according to checklist.

Lessons Learned:

Be vigilant and observant during every stage of the pre-flight and flight operations. It is critical to thoroughly check all systems and equipment before takeoff and to pay close attention to any changes in engine performance or behavior during the flight.

It is important to always be prepared for unexpected situations and to prioritize safety above all else. Additionally, the story highlights the importance of communication with air traffic control and the need to quickly respond to any problems or emergencies that arise during flight.

NOTES:

GREEN LASER DISTRACTION AT A NIGHT

CASA, 2015

I'm a CFII and was instructing an IFR lesson, we were holding at LUSEY on the missed approach out of ILS 22 MMV and on our outbound leg we were hit by a green laser.

I reported the incident to ATC and idented the transponder, then I turned off the taxi/landing/strobe lights and over flew the laser.

Upon turning off the lights the laser lost us but I could still see where it was coming from.

I over flew it, reported to Portland Approach then turned back on all of the lights. Upon turning on the lights, the laser found us again.

ATC asked for me to copy the phone number for the Port of Portland Police and to call them. I called them and made a report, then Portland TRACON called me back. We spoke and they asked me to call the Sheriff in McMinnville.

I did and gave them the best description that I could of where the laser could have come from.

Lessons Learned:

I realized after the fact that I may have broken a rule in turning off my taxi/landing/strobe lights while flying at night. That was not my intention, my intention was solely to remove myself as a visible target for the laser.

I was in Radar contact and knew that I was the only aircraft in the area, so I didn't think that there was a hazard in me turning my taxi/landing/strobe lights off, but while it made me harder for the laser operator to see, it made me harder for other aircraft to see.

I realize that what I should have done was just immediately vacated the area and put the laser on my tail which is how I plan to conduct myself henceforth.

NOTES:

POOR CROSSWIND TECHNIQUE

CASA, 2017

Up to this point, I would estimate that the flight had been entirely normal and conducted with a high degree of precision to both navigation and operational procedures. I mention this because it has been my long held belief that by following the rules and regulations to the letter, or as close as my capabilities allow, then there is a wide margin of options in case of error or emergency.

As I was nearing 2 miles out or so, Tower asked me to turn to the numbers as #2. As I had the previous plane in sight, I acknowledged and started that maneuver. I was around 100 knots, so I had to slow up to put in the first degree of flaps. I then focused to altitude and bringing the plane at about a 45 degree angle to the numbers on Runway 29. I was thinking of gentle turns so as not to induce any need for cross-control or spin close to the ground. I believe the landing was smooth, and the next thing I remember was that the plane was veering to the left edge of the runway. It was leaning with the left wing low. This was my chief concern as I was trying to get it level, which I managed to do.

At that point, I felt I was nearly halfway across the grass to Taxiway Echo. Since a passing plane was well off to the left, I requested Tower to continue through the grass onto Taxiway Echo. They granted this request. I applied enough power, held the attitude so there was less weight on the front tire, and got back onto Taxiway Echo.

Lessons Learned:

I believe the whole incident began when I acknowledged direct to the numbers. I had practiced emergency situations like this earlier this year, both with my CFI and once solo, and felt it was within my capability to do so. This might be true under calm winds, but I forgot to account for the crosswind that would already be needed for a regular, straight-in landing. This poor decision making was my first error. Even though I slowed the plane down for the first degree of flaps, I became so focused on directional control and landing that I made more mistakes, which led to the mishap. First, I never added any more flaps, as my mind focused on making the runway. It was NOT an emergency landing without power but one with power. Second, I forgot to account for the basic cross-wind once I was close to the runway. I was just focused on reaching the numbers. I believe this can be summarized by saying that I was NOT in my normal, stabilized approach. My thinking appeared as if I was applying what I learned for emergencies into the situation when I was still at full power. Thus, it is highly likely that I landed at a higher than usual speed with mis-configured flaps and the wrong cross-wind configurations. As I departed the runway, my major concern was to avoid flipping the plane. At least the decisions after I was already in the grass proved successful in preventing an accident at the cost of a high level of embarrassment.

NOTES:

CHAPTER 5

COMMUNICATION & AIR CREW

"Flying is like good music: it elevates the spirit and it's an exhilarating freedom. It's not a thrill thing or an adrenaline rush; it's engaging in a process that takes focus and commitment. I love the machines, I love the aviation community."

Harrison Ford, Actor and 172 Owner

LISTENING OUT ON THE WRONG FREQUENCY

ASRS, 2019

On a last minute evening flight with a student, we encountered more than we bargained for on our routine training flight. We took off and went out to the practice area to do ground reference maneuvers. While we were out there, we heard two experimental aircraft in the same general area and heard when they switched to a private frequency (to which we placed on our second radio for monitoring purposes.) During our entire training session we were passively listening to the two experimentals out for a fun duo sightseeing flight. We made them aware of our position and the three of us stayed apart from each other.

When we were done with our lesson, we headed back for the airport making all applicable position reports on the CTAF (we do not have a tower). We eventually entered the pattern and flew the downwind and base with no issue. We were still monitoring the second frequency and could hear the two aircraft were still on the other side of the mountain, roughly 9 miles away, so we considered them no factor.

We did not hear anyone else on the CTAF and did not see any other traffic. We turned final for runway XX and I decided to have the student land without flaps because we had been going too fast to put the flaps down and I decided it would be a good opportunity to review landing without flaps. We approached short final at 70-80 MPH (we were in an older 172) and I was so focused on the approach and explaining the visual difference of the touchdown and how it would feel different in ground effect, I never thought to look at the final approach area of the short, rarely used crosswind runway (Runway XY). Winds were calm and we were using the designated calm wind runway. As we were about to cross the approach area of Runway 30, I saw a plane at the same altitude coming at us from the left (he appeared in the pilot side left window). I had enough time to say "PLANE!" and push the yoke forward. We passed underneath the little experimental airplane roughly 10-15 feet. I could clearly see the plane as we went below. The ground was roughly 20-30 feet below us because after pushing underneath I felt the ground effect. We continued in ground effect and decided to abort our landing and head out to the west to figure out what was going on. At this point, I was thinking that was one of the party of two experimental aircraft that I had been monitoring on our second comm. I could not figure out how I didn't hear them return to the airport.

We turned around about 8 miles away and then came back and re-entered the traffic pattern with much caution and landed safely. Upon entering the FBO, the pilot of the rogue airplane was waiting for us. He looked like he'd seen a ghost and immediately began apologizing. I asked him why he was apologizing and he said that it had been him that was landing on Runway XY, that he had been on the wrong frequency, and that he did not see us until we were underneath him. He said he had been on [a discrete frequency] instead of the CTAF. He could not believe the mistake. I could tell he was very sorry. My student and I accepted his apology and then said that we should have been looking for traffic better and we were also at fault for failing to do so.

We had become so focused on the radio traffic, and had been so complacent thinking we were alone in the pattern that we never looked at the approach for that crosswind runway when we were far away from it. The other pilot said he would be much more observant when setting his radio in the future.

Lessons Learned:

It turned out that the two experimental aircraft we had been monitoring were in fact 9-10 miles away like they had reported, and the third aircraft had been floating around the area thinking he was broadcasting on the CTAF and we did not even know the third aircraft was in the vicinity. He had departed 5 minutes before we did, and returned at the same time. The flight lasted [one] hour.

After the fiasco, I mistakenly called out one of the party planes asking him if he had seen us as we flew underneath him. He seemed shocked and said he had not seen us. It was a case of mistaken identity. He had really not seen us because he had never come close to the airport region. His aircraft looks identical to the one we went underneath, so I made an erroneous assumption--what's that saying about making assumptions? I had to apologize to the mistaken identity pilot right after the wrong frequency pilot apologized to me.

The entire scenario could have been prevented if the wrong frequency pilot had been on the correct frequency (1) and if I had been looking for aircraft that may not have radios (2).

NOTES:

HIGH COMMS FAILURE

ASRS, 2018

I was acting as CFI on a flight Review Flight for a certified Private Pilot with an Instrument rating. [The pilot] was acting as PIC for the whole flight and operating radios. As CFI I was having him perform required tasks for a flight review and to get him current. Upon returning to ZZZ our point of departure PIC unintentionally performed touch and go on 28R when Tower had cleared him to land on 28L. Both PIC and CFI were shocked that somehow we had missed the correct clearance. Upon landing PIC called [the Tower] and gave his name and phone number.

I, as CFI, proceeded to research the situation further by pulling up the ATC recording to determine where miscommunication happened, that led to a possible pilot deviation under my supervision.

Initial Call by PIC - [pilot] requests landing with information. Initial Tower Response - make straight in 28R. I inform PIC to correct his call and asked him to request touch and goes. PIC requested touch and goes.

No initial response from Tower due to traffic load. A minute later Tower asked, "Who asked for touch and goes?" PIC responds [with abbreviated tail number].

No immediate response from the Tower. Eventually, Tower responds with a clearance for [a similar abbreviated call sign] #2 Cleared touch and Go 28R. PIC flying responds #2 Cleared touch and go 28R. An incorrect call by PIC responding to a clearance for a similar sounding tail number. As CFI I did not hear the initial call sign only the [letter]. There was no correction by the Tower that PIC read back wrong clearance for a similar sounding tail number. PIC proceeds to line up for touch and go on 28R.

On short final Tower gives clearance [with full call sign to] make short final cleared to Land 28L. PIC responds Cleared to land. As CFI I did not hear the Tower give 28L due to congested and blocked communication. The student gave incomplete clearance read back without runway assignment. Tower did not respond to correct and requesting full clearance read back.

PIC continued to perform touch and go on 28R upon turning right crosswind to downwind, Tower told PIC that next time he did a go-around he needed to communicate his intentions. It was apparent Tower was unaware of landing on the wrong runway or where we were until on right downwind for 28R.

Upon the confusion, CFI took the radio and asked Tower to clarify clearance. Tower confirmed clearance was to land on 28L. PIC received clearance to land on 28R, upon which was given a number for the Tower due to the possible pilot deviation.

Lessons Learned:

What I believe caused this possible deviation? Multiple errors by PIC, CFI, and Tower.

Due to heavy congested airspace, radio communications, and incomplete and wrong radio calls that went uncorrected by Tower.

- Errors by Pilot: Reading Back incorrect and incomplete clearances. Not asking for clarification when airspace and radio were busy.
- Errors by CFI: Failure to ask Tower for clarification for clearance amidst busy and congested pattern and radio communications. As CFI my attention was outside the aircraft scanning for traffic which took my attention away from clearly hearing the communications when my student made incorrect and wrong read backs.
- Errors by Tower: Initial clearance was given for straight in 28R. According to ATC recordings, next to actual clearance that was given when we were already lined up short final 28R. This clearance was given late and appeared Tower had lost [the aircraft] amidst busy pattern. Tower also failed to correct PIC's wrong clearance for #2 Cleared to land 28R miles earlier, and failure to have PIC read back full clearance with runway number.

The problem was a miscommunication and misunderstanding of clearance between PIC, CFI, and Tower due to task saturation, busy airspace, and busy communications.

What will be done to correct the situation?

As the CFI, I will take more diligence to maintain a sterile cockpit when providing instruction to clarify clearances when there is any doubt or miscommunication. When airspace and communications are busy I will use extreme caution and take extra time to listen to clearances even when flying with certified pilots. I will provide my student further instruction concerning Radio Communications and Clearances, Airport Operations, Runway Incursions, Traffic Avoidance.

As to the Tower, often ZZZ gets extremely busy with 2 parallel runways in use. Many of the flights in and out of ZZZ are due to flight instruction.

As a result communication with Tower becomes extremely difficult, with calls often being missed, stepped on, and miscommunicated. It has been a procedure by ZZZ Tower to split the two runways on different frequencies. In my opinion, the split of frequencies should have occurred when a single Tower operator started missing calls.

Upon our downwind leg for final landing on 28R the Tower then decided to split the runway frequencies. If this had been done earlier it would have been easier for PIC, CFI, and Tower to communicate and clarify the correct clearance.

NOTES:

DISORIENTED FLIGHT
INSTRUCTOR

ASRS, 2018

My CFI and I departed in daylight VMC to practice the VOR RWY 5 Approach at ZZZ2 on an instrument training flight - simulated partial panel.

After shooting the approach, it was getting dark. My CFII gave me a heading, tuned the localizer for ZZZ1, and instructed me to practice tracking the localizer at 3,000 feet while he got the current ATIS at ZZZ. It appeared that he was getting us set up to return home to ZZZ.

My CFII asked me to look up over my view-limiting device to see ZZZ1's runway, which I did, and then resume tracking toward ZZZ1 at 3,000 feet while he would get us set up to return to home base (ZZZ). My CFII called ZZZ Tower and reported inbound (4 or 5 mile straight in).

We executed positive exchange of controls to my CFII so that I could remove my view-limiting device, and he initiated a descent.

I confirmed vocally that the airplane was still his, as he continued to descend, but was not verbally communicating his intentions/plan to me. ZZZ Tower asked our altitude, and my CFII responded 1,500 feet or 1,600 feet.

Tower said he was worried we were in ZZZ1's airspace and asked my CFII if we knew where we were. It was at this time that the situation deteriorated and my CFII froze. He confessed he did not know where he or the airport was. We were getting low and slow and CFII kept repeating he didn't know where we were, but did not take corrective action; I declared "my airplane, I am PIC" with positive exchange of controls acknowledgment from my CFII ("Ok, you are PIC") and verbalized that I was climbing to a safe altitude and navigating accordingly.

I requested radar vectors from to ZZZ, and was asked if I had an instructor on board. I said yes I have an instructor on board but he is 'turned around,' e.g. disoriented and confused. ZZZ Tower offered me to go over to ZZZ Approach for vectors to final. I accepted and contacted ZZZ. I requested a safe altitude and heading to fly, as I could see traffic outside and knew two other airports and mountains were in close vicinity and it was night. They gave me a heading and altitude to maintain and asked how much fuel I had on board. I confirmed at least an hour's worth of fuel remaining, but that I needed to land.

I was unable to tell whether my instructor was disoriented/panic attack or something else and believe the safety of the flight necessitated this prompt corrective action. ZZZ asked me which approach I would like, and I requested the ILS because I am most familiar with that approach and it is a precision approach. They gave me vectors to intercept the localizer which I did, confirmed I had the runway in sight, and Approach asked if we would need assistance on the ground. I asked my CFII if he was okay and he said no assistance, so I responded "Negative" and switched to advisory (ZZZ Tower) when instructed by Approach. ZZZ Tower cleared me to land and I landed uneventfully.

Lessons Learned:

CFII not communicating intentions/plan with student, lack of initial corrective action upon disorientation at night, loss of situational awareness, and not talking to ATC are human performance considerations that contributed to this chain of events.

NOTES:

LOSING COMMUNICATIONS ON A SOLO FLIGHT

ASRS, 2018

Narrative: 1

The issue occurred during my solo cross country flight, my flight plan was to fly at/between 3,500 and 3,000 feet cross the mountains maintaining VFR and return to 3,000/3,500 feet once I got over the mountains [to] avoid airspace, and maintain VFR and stay under the clouds, to avoid terrible turbulence. I had to deviate course some to do this.

While on this flight I experienced communications failure with Center and could not get in touch with anyone. Being a student pilot, without communications, and flying into a major airport I considered this to be an emergency situation.

As I was crossing over [a] Class D airspace at 3,500 feet I encountered a regional jet that was to my right going south to north as I was going east to west. Without communication and without a way to get in touch or make sure he knew where I was I dropped altitude to avoid the regional jet.

While landing there was a crosswind coming across the field. As I went to land straight down the middle there was a strong gust of wind that blew me from the middle of the runway to the far left of the runway when I was 5 to 10 feet off the ground. I managed to keep the plane level put when I landed my left wheel pulled to the left and without flipping the plane was unable to correct and I struck a runway light.

Narrative: 2

I endorsed one of my student pilots to make a direct trip in a Cessna 172.

The student had previously received training in flight following as well as landing in a controlled environment.

On the trip in question the pilot intermittently lost contact with Center while receiving flight following, causing him to miss calls from [Center] as well as him not responding to call from [Center].

Lessons Learned:

Narrative: 1

To correct these actions I have ensured that avionics in the plane have been checked to ensure the loss of communications would not occur again. And to avoid the crosswind gust will ensure to practice landings to a high standard.

Narrative: 2

I believe that the cause of the issue was the pilot's altitude in combination with our radio system that interferes with him continuing to maintain contact. That loss in contact may have caused him to pass through Class C and D airspace without making contact.

To prevent this from happening again I will provide cross country training along the route of flight my student's plan to fly on their solo cross country flights. I will also be providing additional training in the radio systems and backup systems before allowing solo flight to continue.

NOTES:

UNACCEPTABLE LOSS OF SITUATIONAL AWARENESS

ASRS, 2018

An instrument student and I, a CFI-I, were performing an IFR training flight on an active flight plan to review approach procedures.

After completing our first approach, the ILS runway 19 approach, we executed the prescribed missed approach procedures by flying a 160 heading and beginning a climb up to 3,000 feet.

After contacting approach, we received instruction to climb to 4,000 feet and were told to expect vectors (as requested) to the VOR runway 28 approach. Within a few minutes, we were given a "downwind" vector towards the approach course.

We continued to fly for approximately 15 miles away from the airport/VORTAC at 4,000 feet, and our "downwind" was farther away from the airport than is typical for this approach. Before I had the chance to query ATC about our distance, we were given a base turn, and shortly thereafter a heading and instruction to intercept the final approach course.

At this point, according to track log data from FlightAware, we were still about 18 miles away from the airport. Within the next few miles, we were given the instruction "10 miles from the VOR, Cleared VOR RWY 28 Approach". My student began descending from 4,000 feet to the published at-or-above altitude of 2,300 feet that was applicable for the straight-in approach prior to the FAF. During the descent, we broke out of the cloud layer at approximately 3,200 feet.

Within a minute or so of going visual, I noticed that our GPS indicated that we were just passing 10 miles from the VOR and we were level at an altitude of 2,300 feet.

Now, on the VOR RWY 28, the published approach course associated with the 2,300 foot step-down/at-or-above altitude states "remain within 10 miles" in reference to the procedure turn completion altitude of 3,300 feet, after which an aircraft performing the "full approach" would re-intercept the inbound course and descend to 2,300 feet. Upon realizing our remaining distance to the VOR, I became concerned that we had descended too low (the applicable MSA prescribes 3,600 feet) for that area of the approach and had descended to the 2,300 feet step-down prematurely (prior to within 10mi of the VOR), placing the aircraft in potential conflict with obstructions and terrain.

Subsequent analysis of the FlightAware track-log clearly shows my aircraft below the 3,600 MSA at distances greater than 10 miles from the VOR which, within 10 miles, a descent to 2,300 would have been otherwise completely safe.

While ATC had implied in our clearance that we were within 10 miles of the VOR, and after we descended made no subsequent mention of our altitude (which may have been perfectly safe in reference to their MVA for that sector as we regularly transit that area at such lower altitudes when receiving vectors), as PIC it was still my responsibility to ensure compliance with all MSA's and step-down altitudes on the approach.

Lessons Learned:

Ultimately, my failing to confirm the controller's guidance regarding our aircraft's position and blindly descending on that information represents an unacceptable loss of situational awareness on my part, and it may have put our otherwise uneventful training flight in highly unnecessary and completely avoidable danger.

Moving forward, it is necessary to confirm and, when applicable, query ATC when receiving a position report in conjunction with an approach clearance to keep an eye on the big picture and maintain situational awareness.

Also, a better understanding of "when and how far can I descend if cleared..." relating to this scenario dealing with this approach (which, in all other times I have used the procedure, I have been vectored within 10 miles of the station) would have increased my awareness that our descent was premature and hazardous.

NOTES:

CHAPTER 6
WEATHER & WIND

"The high wing placement in the 172 makes it a great photo reconnaissance platform."

Brandon Webb
    Former Navy SEAL & Pilot

A GUSTY WIND BLOWS

ASRS, 2015

This evening, I decided to take off from my airport (SFZ), visit a nearby VOR, and return. It was intended as a quick, easy flight.

Warning signs about the day manifested itself with a call. The WX briefer mentioned that there was an AIRMET for moderate turbulence below 8,000 as well as an urgent PIREP for low level wind shear at an airport about 30 NM away. Winds at North Central (SFZ) were 33014G21KT. These were right down one of our two runways, and I was seeking out more challenging conditions to push my personal minimums.

The line worker told me "good luck with those winds" as she was fueling my airplane. I told her that they were right down the runway and she agreed with a "yeah, I guess so. I guess you should be okay."

After preflight and taxi, I started my run-up. I noticed that the plane was really getting buffeted on the ground by the winds and I thought to myself, "This is rather windy."

I considered turning around but told myself that I came this far and I may as well fly, with the stipulation that if I felt uncomfortable while airborne I would return immediately. I finished my run-up and took off.

I climbed to about 2,000 feet or so and was on my way to the Putnam VOR. Almost immediately after passing 1,000 feet I started to experience moderate turbulence. Shortly after the plane banked 30 degrees to the left in under a second without me changing any flight controls. I decided to abort my flight immediately.

A 180 degree set me up for a 45 entry to 33. Due to the winds the plane was essentially ground-tracking sideways. The sensation was that of not flying forward but instead to the side with a massive crab. This spooked me, and this is where my questionable aeronautical decision making of taking off turning into a poor decision. My base for 33 was so unusual and I was feeling so uncomfortable with the situation that I decided to climb and join the pattern for the longer, wider runway 23.

At this point, I both consciously and subconsciously just wanted to get on the ground. I was finding myself in somewhat unusual attitudes while fighting to maintain altitude, and the AWOS was now reporting winds variable between 270 and 350 13G27... a 15 knot gust factor with unpredictable winds. An experienced professional pilot may have had no problems with this, but I am not that pilot. I was determined to get on the ground but also scared. What I should have done was abort the approach to 33, overfly the field on the upwind, and reenter the pattern and try again. Instead, I decided to switch to the wider, "safer" runway. Instead of having a gusty, wind-shear-prone approach with winds right down the runway, they were now giving me a direct crosswind with all the same wind-related problems. Keep in mind that my Skyhawk has a max demonstrated crosswind component of 15 knots; I was now becoming the proverbial "test pilot".

Predictably, my approach was very poor.

Approach speed in my 172 is 75MPH with flaps up and 70MPH with flaps down; I was approaching with 100MPH with 10 degrees in. I knew this as well and instead of going around, I said to myself "I have 7,000 feet(!) of runway; I will float down the runway for a considerable period of time so let it float and it'll come down when it's ready."

There are two problems with this line of reasoning: I didn't have 7,000 feet, I had 5,000, and that crosswind had a slight tailwind component to it as well.

As predicted, I floated for what seemed like a very long time. Finally, the wheels came down, but I started porpoising. I let it bounce a few times, hoping to let it settle, but the end of the runway was fast approaching. After four bounces I executed a sloppy go-around in which I forgot to turn off the carb heat. There's a church that we are supposed to use as a noise abatement landmark that indicates we can make turns at 1,450 feet MSL... I was at 750 feet MSL by the time I was over the church. The airport altitude is around 50 MSL.

Thankfully, my training regarding avoiding power-on stalls and spins by not pitching up aggressively and utilizing heavy right rudder on takeoff prevented me from making a poor situation even worse.

After gaining my composure I set up for a base entry to runway 33, like I should have in the first place. I was able to set up a respectable approach to 33, landed the airplane, and put in an urgent PIREP very shortly after tying down.

Lessons Learned:

I am very fortunate to be able to submit this report right now.

I ventured forth into conditions that I thought I could handle and those conditions turned out to be beyond what I can handle at this stage in my private aviation career. I made a series of poor decisions regarding bad Aeronautical Decision Making (ADM).

Specifically, go/no-go, subpar runway selection and sloppy go-around technique that could have very easily bent metal or worse, ended up with me killing myself. This all happened within the span of 30 minutes. I intend on talking with an instructor regarding this experience and to fix my go-around technique, and hopefully I will avoid situations like this in the future.

NOTES:

DEPARTING IN MARGINAL CONDITIONS

ASRS, 2015

We departed on a personal flight from Airport ZZZ. The ceilings were reported to be 1,900 feet MSL, and that was confirmed on our climb. Previously I had checked the weather both on my phone and at the computer at the FBO and found ceilings were 1,900 feet, but the ceilings were looking lower to the north.

I did not get an official weather briefing, which was a mistake. I also did not get a briefing from an actual person which may have delayed my flight. The satellite picture showed improving skies [90 NM] to the north along our intended route.

We previously had flown into ZZZ from the south and the reported ceilings of 1,900 feet MSL were confirmed. We managed to stay below the clouds, but at times it was stressful and difficult. This led me to believe that we could again stay below the clouds VFR until the skies cleared to the north.

Our takeoff was uneventful. We managed to fly 20 miles north of ZZZ before the overcast clouds started forcing us down.

Suddenly my GPS went into terrain warning mode displaying numerous towers in our path. [At 30 NM north] I noticed terrain increasing in height and made the decision to turn immediately 180 degrees back to ZZZ but it was too late. After initiating the turn, we were completely in IMC.

I tried to stay calm and initiated a climb to the east getting on the gauges. I maintained wings level and tried to hold my heading on east as closely as possible. I resisted panic and thought about declaring an emergency, but I felt I had to maintain aircraft control over anything else. I made constant changes to aircraft while scanning gauges and resisting both vertigo and spatial disorientation.

After about ten minutes or so we managed to climb into clear VFR conditions on top at 5,500 feet MSL and proceeded to the northeast, [diverting to ZZZ1].

Lessons Learned:

My overconfidence in the weather clearing and disregard of potential consequences led to the flight which nearly cost me my life and the lives of my family members who were on board. In retrospect I should have stayed on the ground until the ceilings improved but I was anxious to get home after flying all day and I was overcome with wishful thinking.

I should have gotten an in-person weather briefing which would have likely persuaded me to stay on the ground.

From now on I will set personal minimums in terms of ceilings in which I will fly VFR and will finish my IFR rating which I have not completed.

NOTES:

CLIMBING THROUGH CLOUDS
WITHOUT RATING

ASRS, 2017

I was at ZZZ airport, preparing to depart for ZZZ1 airport, but the weather forecast had deteriorated to low ceilings and mountain obscuration for the first part of the route. We decided to take off, realizing that we might have to return.

As we flew, it quickly became apparent that the entire mountain range we had to cross was obscured. We landed back at ZZZ, went inside and reviewed the weather, noticing that the satellites showed thinner coverage was about to pass overhead. We went outside, noticed breaks in the cloud coverage. At this point, I had an airport return deadline and my passenger needed to be back as well. We were very close to being late.

We started up and I contacted ground, asking for a climb to "VFR on top". Ground control caught me by surprise by issuing me a clearance that sounded a lot like an IFR clearance which rattled me a little because I don't have an IFR rating in airplanes, only helicopters.

I didn't realize until landing later in the day and looking it up that the correct term for what I was looking for was "VFR over the top", not "VFR on top", which is an IFR clearance.

Feeling a little confused, I went along and fortunately, ground called me back shortly and said it was denied by approach. I felt relieved but a little shaken up because I suspected that I had just requested an IFR clearance without an IFR rating.

We took off, left East to class E airspace and began climbing to the cloud gaps that we had noticed to get over the clouds and beyond the coastal mountain range to clear skies.

As we circled to climb toward the gaps, it appeared that everything was fine but at about 5,000 feet, I realized that we weren't going to be able to climb fast enough to make it over the clouds.

Looking right and left, I realized that the clouds, which had appeared to have plenty of room at first, were actually closing in and if we turned, we ran the risk of going IMC with most of the cloud layer to pass through on our way down.

Looking up, I realized that the shortest route to safety was up. Our climb to the top was over in about 20-30 seconds and didn't involve much time in the clouds but it was a long 20 seconds because I realized the situation that I was in was in violation of the FARs.

Lessons Learned:

As far as human factors go, I know that my deadline and my passenger's commitment influenced my tolerance for risking the climb-out as well as my desire to get home rather than staying another night.

Also, the fact that we had already tried to depart once played a role because I felt like we would be trapped if we didn't try to climb out VFR.

In addition, my exchange with the controller shook me up a little which left me feeling defensive about what I was doing.

That contributed to continuing with my obviously poor decision to try to climb out VFR.

Another contributing factor was my poor judgment of climb performance which is probably because I only have about 30 hours in the Cessna 172.

The remainder of my airplane time is in the 182 which has a little better performance.

NOTES:

IFR IN THE CLOUDS

ASRS, 2017

I was on an IFR flight plan. I descended into the clouds at about 5500 feet, and was cleared for the ILS 11 approach. Bases were reported at 600'. Minimums for the approach were 200'. I was given instructions to maintain 3000' until established.

This was my first time flying an approach in this particular aircraft, and it only had a single axis autopilot (my usual aircraft has dual axis).

I intercepted the inbound course high above the glidepath and started to descend. Within a minute, I noted that I was high above the glidepath and I was too close to the airport to continue to safely descend, so I executed the missed approach and informed ATC that I needed to try again.

Mistake #1 that set up the rest of this flight... As I reviewed the initial error with my radar track (later on the ground), I realize now that ATC had likely intended and expected me to fly the full approach with a procedure turn.

I thought I was being given a direct intercept to the final approach course, so I did not fly the full approach the first time, and that is why I was too high.

After this initial missed approach, I accepted another clearance for the full approach with procedure turn. That approach and one more subsequent approach also ended in missed approaches with my altitude too high. As I was hand flying the aircraft for much of the time, I misread the chart and did not realize that I should have been descending to 1300′ before glideslope intercept.

On one attempt, ATC offered a DME arc as an alternative as it would have given me a more natural intercept without requiring a quick descent from 3000 to 1300′. I declined this offer, as I did not want to reprogram the GPS while hand flying in IMC.

At one point, I may have become slightly disoriented while hand flying, and I had to recover from a slight unusual attitude in IMC. I engaged the autopilot in ROL mode to regain my bearings. I noted that the CDI and Glideslope indicator seemed to jump in and out on occasion, and the autopilot would not accurately track the inbound course in either APR or NAV mode. I had to hand fly.

I declined the offer of a VFR alternate from ATC, as the closest VFR airport was 200 miles away. I would not have had enough fuel to fly there.

On my final attempt at an approach, I decided to descend below the clouds as much as possible while still over water so that I could establish visual reference with the ground without risk of obstructions.

I intentionally descended below the glidepath while following my course on Foreflight so that I could establish contact with the ground. I did break out and establish contact with the ground, and I followed the CDI to the airport.

ATC gave me a low altitude warning and instructed me to climb to 3000′. I declined, and let them know that I had the airport in sight. Visibility was good below the clouds.

Lessons Learned:

This entire ordeal had at least two human causes. My initial expectation of a direct approach caused the initial missed approach. My subsequent stress of hand flying in IMC caused me to misread the chart and remain too high to intercept on the next two approaches.

I overcorrected my course adjustments, and never stabilized on any approach. I initially expected this to be an easy garden variety ILS approach, and was not prepared for hand flying an unfamiliar airplane in IMC.

<u>NOTES:</u>

OPERATION IN IMC CONDITIONS WITHOUT A RATING

ASRS, 2018

When I was on my flight to ZZZ airport, I noticed clouds and precipitation to the south/southwest, that's when I listened to ZZZ1 airport ASOS. It had said that there was no precipitation and clouds were still high.

When I got the clearance to come into ZZZ airport on a right base leg for Runway XX, it was clear to see that there were haze and mist to the south/southeast. My original plan was to do a full stop taxi back Runway XX. Given the weather I saw coming, I decided to park and go into the FBO to check the weather again.

I saw on radar through 1800wxbrief.com that a storm was passing through. I checked the METARs and they were saying clouds 6,000 feet overcast and 7sm visibility. I decided to take off; I got to 2,300 feet MSL to see that visibility was around 3sm, I decided to come back to ZZZ to land. Tower even said they had lost sight of me when I was on base leg to final Runway XX.

I landed and parked the plane again and looked at the radar.

It showed a massive storm directly to my south going northeast and a small storm about to hit and soon pass. I made the decision to refuel and preflight at ZZZ so when I did get the pocket to leave I could do it without wasting time. My next stop was planned for ZZZ2 airport.

I looked at METARs from ZZZ to ZZZ2 and forecasts, ZZZ2 showed it was 6,000 foot overcast and 10sm visibility. ZZZ was reporting overcast 6,000 foot clouds, mist, and 4sm visibility. I could clearly see that visibility was less and I proceeded to wait until the storm had passed until I got my pocket of clarity.

I had discussed my plan with my Flight Instructor and he saw what was happening on radar and METARs forecasted for ZZZ, ZZZ2, and ZZZ3. He agreed with my plan and said once I get the visibility and clouds I need to get out of there. When I noticed it was clearing up and visibility was clearing, I called a weather briefer and he told me the same thing as the METARs, he advised me to be very careful on my flight.

Going into the flight, I knew I had to be cautious because of the visibility, clouds, and higher elevation due to hilly terrain. I departed ZZZ and activated my VFR flight plan from ZZZ to ZZZ2. I had planned to cruise at 4,500 feet giving me enough room to be below the overcast clouds. Visibility was at 5sm with haze/mist mixture, any lower I would've turned around immediately and probably would have spent the night at ZZZ.

ZZZ Tower had put me on flight following to ZZZ2 with the intention of doing a touch and go and departing immediately to ZZZ4. ZZZ Tower transferred me to ATC Radio. For the first 15 minutes of my flight to ZZZ2 visibility was clearing to 10sm and clouds at 6,000 feet. I could clearly see a massive shelf cloud that was not forecast to my northeast going east. I could clearly see the ground below to check off my VFR checkpoints.

When I reached 4,500 feet I had noticed the shelf cloud to be below me, so I stayed at 4,500 feet. When I reached my third VFR checkpoint that's when I saw clouds had moved in behind and to both sides of me.

At that time as well, ATC Radio had transferred me to ATC Center. I told ATC Center, [I was at 4,500ft]. We had radar contact, shortly after I told them there were clouds ahead of me and I didn't know what to do, I needed help. The shelf cloud looked to be 3,000 feet to 6,000 feet. I had lost sight of the ground due to fog as well. As I was looking for ground or an opening, I ended up going into the cloud.

I notified ATC Center and told them I was not IFR rated, and that I was now in the cloud for a total time of 10 seconds. I knew I was in a cloud because as I looked outside the cockpit it was a complete whiteout and I was surrounded. When I was in the cloud, I immediately looked at my instruments keeping my heading and altitude the same and made sure to not panic or move around to get disoriented.

When I got out of the cloud, I could clearly see a few clouds ahead of me and I had broken FAR 91.155 basic VFR weather minimums, being in class E airspace. I also checked periodically to make sure there was no icing on the wings.

Right after I got out of the cloud, I asked about ZZZ2 weather and they said visibility was roughly 1sm or 1.5sm, that's when I decided to divert towards ZZZ4. I immediately put into the GPS so I knew exactly where I was going and asked if I could descend from 4,500 feet to 4,000 feet to get below the clouds ahead of me.

I knew the clouds would end shortly because ATC Center had told me a local PIREP stating it was 10sm visibility and 6,000 feet overcast. Again, I looked around the surrounding area and there were still clouds behind, left, right, and now ahead of me. Also, it was heavy fog and haze below me.

ATC Center asked if I could see the ground or dodge the clouds because they needed 2 miles to figure out a better plan for me, I responded and said that it was patchy below me and I could stay away from the clouds.

I asked if I could descend again to 3,800 feet cruising altitude, they responded with altitude was at my discretion, just to try and stay on a constant heading. They came back and said to stay on course to ZZZ4 airport and altitude at my discretion.

During the duration of the time I was talking to ATC Center, I asked if they could change my VFR flight plan from ZZZ to ZZZ2, to ZZZ to ZZZ4. They responded and said they had already changed it. The clouds started to break, there was still heavy fog below me that I could see ending and overcast of 11,000 feet as was forecast from ZZZ3 METAR. The fog below was curved and looked to be ending halfway in-between when I diverted and ZZZ3 airport. At that point, ATC Center had transferred me to ZZZ3 Approach.

I contacted ZZZ3 Approach, [and advised them I was at 3,600 feet]. I had lowered my altitude after the break of heavy fog. ATC responded with two-way communication and radar contact. Also, it started to get darker, so I decided to turn on my navigation lights to ensure anyone around me could see me.

When I got closer to their airspace, they told [me] to cruise at 3,500 feet. Then they told me to fly VFR at my discretion and to have a good flight. Between the cloud break and when I landed at ZZZ4, my flight was smooth no turbulence, no clouds, 10sm visibility, and clouds at 11,000 ft. overcast. I entered ZZZ4 entry corridors and landed smoothly. When I shut down, I closed my flight plan and reviewed the flight with my Flight Instructor.

Lessons Learned:

The contributing factors of the flight were unexpected weather that no METAR or TAF was forecasting and reporting.

I checked all my resources before taking off from ZZZ airport before I left. The leg from ZZZ to ZZZ2 is limited in weather reporting systems. The corrective actions I made was choosing to wait the first time from ZZZ and ultimately diverting to ZZZ4.

Also, I changed my attitude to better understand what the clouds were and to make appropriate judgment calls based on what I saw.

My concerns were that I was breaking a regulation in an impossible situation, not being able to go anywhere without going through clouds, and how unexpected and fast moving the clouds were.

I was not worried about going into the cloud because ATC Center was watching me on the radar, I was actively talking to them, and my instrument simulated training in the past had kept my head steady.

I believe to ensure to not have a re-occurrence of what happened during this flight, is to stay at the airport on the ground until you know for sure all weather conditions are well above minimums.

NOTES:

NIGHT FLYING VFR WAS REALLY IFR

ASRS, 2018

I successfully convinced myself that at night, if there's any weather at all, I should be in on an instrument flight plan.

I arrived at SQL having picked up an IFR clearance en route because the weather was reported as marginal, but on arrival into the Bay Area, things were almost totally clear south of OAK. I waited for a passenger for about 30-45 minutes before departing back to the east.

I chose not to pick up an IFR clearance for the return flight because it had been clear on the way in and the weather reports weren't any different. We departed VFR and began a slow climb underneath the SFO Bravo shelves to get out past Sunol Grade when we began to contact the bases around 1,800-2,000 feet. I descended back to 1,500 feet and worked south towards RHV for a little while thinking I had just picked a bad spot.

At some point near VPNUM it felt as if the clouds were descending and the terrain was rising, and having read a lot of reports of other people making this mistake.

I made an immediate 180 and decided to return to Palo Alto to land and pick up an IFR clearance. I was listening to but not talking to Norcal, who had been really busy on my approach, and believe but have not confirmed they cannot issue new clearances that low over the bay due to MVAs?

Also, I decided it was safer to be on the ground copying a clearance rather than trying to navigate at night with lowering layers, complex airspace, and low altitude.

On the return to PAO I started off direct before almost blundering into NUQ's airspace although I believe I avoided it by maybe half a mile. In the end, landed safely at PAO, called Norcal for a clearance from the ground, and continued on our flight IFR and much more comfortably.

Lessons Learned:

Lessons worth learning: Marginal VFR at night is 100% IFR worthy, even if you have to deal with more complicated clearance delivery.

NUQ's airspace, where it intersects with PAO's, continues to confuse me.

NOTES:

FAILURE OF VHF IN IMC

ASRS, 2014

I took an evening pleasure flight to ZZZ for dinner accompanied by my older brother. I acquired a commercially provided weather briefing prior to departing which advised my route was VFR and forecast to be so until around XA00 local time.

We landed in ZZZ, grabbed dinner and went back to the airport to head back home with 2.5 hours of fuel on board. I quickly rechecked the weather on my tablet computer using a commercial app and nothing had changed.

We took off and departed with a cruising altitude of 5,500 feet indicated.

Enroute the weather quickly turned south. I noticed larger CB clouds forming around me, and a thick cloud deck forming in front of me. I opted to drop my altitude to 3,500 feet indicated to maintain VFR cloud clearance and duck below it.

Once I crossed the river, the weather seemed to open up. I then decided to climb to 5,000 feet to get a better look of what was going on around me.

I executed climbing 360's until I reached 5,000 feet and realized the weather was worse than I thought. It was solid IMC everywhere around me, deteriorating rapidly and it appeared I was in the only VMC conditions around me.

I then started checking different enroute weather services to get a picture of what was going on around me. At this point, I had 1.3 hours of fuel left and realized that any airport within range was heavy IMC conditions with ceilings ranging from 600 to 1,400 feet.

I decided to continue towards [my home airport] using my VOR's to track Victor XXX (I have been doing instrument training the past few months and am fairly familiar with IFR operations in the area. This may have been the wrong move in retrospect but this is what I determined was safest at the time). I maintained 1,000(+/-300feet) feet above the cloud deck for some form of traffic separation, but could not see the ground as it was solid overcast.

Shortly after, both NAV 1 and NAV 2 failed, but DME was still operational. I attempted to radio Center for vectors and help, but to no avail. It appeared my radio could receive but not transmit.

I attempted to navigate back towards [my airport] via my iPad, but the battery died shortly after. At this point, the weather was so poor that flying through clouds became unavoidable.

Shortly after, I was in complete IMC in the clouds. I executed an emergency 180 using my turn coordinator and my stopwatch, and held that heading for a few minutes. Realizing it wasn't improving, I decided to climb to get above the deck once again for traffic separation. I climbed for approximately 20 minutes and popped out above the deck at 10,000 feet indicated. It was solid overcast as far as the eye could see.

Knowing the gravity of the situation, I told my brother to take his phone out and set an alarm for 15 minutes. I didn't tell him the reason as not to alarm him, but I knew if that alarm went off, we had 30 minutes of fuel and I needed to find a place to get down, quick. At this point, I was very disoriented as to where I was, and had no way to call for help.

Using my DME, I determined where I was relative to the tuned VOR/DME by flying different headings, and observing the DME's reaction. I then pulled out my sectional chart, drew a line straight from the VOR, and determined I was roughly 6 miles south of [the airport I took off from].

I then turned direct north and held this heading for 10 more minutes, so as to get far north of the field where I knew there were no obstacles while descending from 10,000 down to 2,000. Once my brother's cell phone got signal, I pulled up a computerized satellite map and used that to line myself up with XXL coming from the north. I then maintained a slow but steady descent as I continued essentially a poor man's GPS approach. I broke through the clouds at roughly 1,200 feet AGL and landed on XXL.

Lessons Learned:

It is important to be well-prepared for a flight, particularly when it comes to weather conditions. Always be prepared for changing weather conditions: Even if the weather forecast is favorable, it can change quickly and unexpectedly. Pilots should always be aware of the weather conditions along their route and be prepared to adjust their plans accordingly.

It's important for pilots to always have a backup plan and be ready to change course if necessary. Plan the divert before you need to.

It underscores the importance of remaining calm under pressure and being able to think creatively and strategically to overcome challenges in flight. It's also a reminder of the critical importance of good training and regular practice, particularly for instrument flying and emergency procedures.

NOTES:

SUSPECTING A MALFUNCTION

ASRS, 2014

The aircraft had just received its annual inspection where it was reported that the loose nose wheel drag link had been shimmed.

After preflight inspection a copilot and I were to fly to a nearby airport for lunch. I was the pilot in command; my copilot was to operate the radios in Class C airspace. Every aspect of the flight into our destination was normal and the aircraft handled well.

After lunch we prepared to return to our home base. The wind was reported 7 KTS at 270 with gust of 14. Once cleared for 18, I began my roll down the runway with wind correction and at 60 I started to rotate.

At this stage, the aircraft violently pulled to the left, the aircraft became airborne; wing level in a high-pitched attitude and a direction 45 degrees left of the runway. Knowing my aircraft had just been worked on, my perception at that moment was I had lost control of both the nose wheel and rudder and an aggressive correction to the right may not be possible or safe.

The aircraft was aligned with Taxiway P, there was no traffic anywhere to be seen, and I decided to abort the takeoff and land on the taxiway.

The Tower was contacted, we declared we had a mishap and wanted to return to the FBO.

At the FBO I telephoned the Tower to explain what had happened. We could not find any obvious fault with the controls on the ground but decided it would be better to hangar the aircraft.

The next day I returned to the airport with a mechanic familiar with my aircraft and a CFI who also was familiar with me in my aircraft. Once the mechanic was satisfied the aircraft was fit to fly I returned to my home base with the CFI and demonstrated an additional two crosswind takeoff and landings.

Lessons Learned:

I believe a gust of wind turned the aircraft.

With the nose high, the wheel steering in a 172 becomes disengaged and the relatively low airspeed made the rudder less effective.

The aggressive turn and lack of response of the rudder or nose wheel to peddle lead me to believe there was a fault.

<u>NOTES:</u>

CHAPTER 7

CONTROLLED AIRSPACE & AIR TRAFFIC CONTROL

"I approached Red Square three times, trying to find somewhere to land, before discovering a wide bridge nearby. I landed there and taxied into Red Square."

Mathias Rust
172 pilot who flew to Russia in 1987

CONFUSION WITH THE CLEARANCE

ASRS, 2017

My student and I were on an IFR clearance, on course and glide path for the BLI ILS RWY 16 final approach segment in simulated IFR conditions, in hazy VMC, overcast at approximately 5,000. There were two VFR airplanes in the vicinity, under control of the BLI tower.

Victoria Terminal instructed my student (pilot flying) to contact Bellingham tower. He changed frequency and reported that we were inbound on the ILS 16. Tower asked us for our distance from the runway; I signalled to my student that we were four miles out (GPS distance was a little more than 4 NM). The Tower then issued instructions to the other two airplanes that seemed to me intended to provide separation before he cleared them behind us. Initially it seemed to me that he was considering sending one of them in front of us, considering our distance from the runway. Tower had also asked my student for our speed, if I recall correctly. One of the VFR airplanes was instructed to execute a "tight 360" and re-enter the base leg for Runway 16.

Victoria Terminal had instructed us to execute the published missed approach, PF told Victoria Terminal that after the missed approach we wanted vectors to return to ZZZ, the next destination on our IFR clearance following BLI. We were not instructed to execute the KIENO Five DP, but assumed vectoring during execution of the missed approach that would send us if not to the KIENO intersection, then to the Penn Cove (CVV) VOR.

On short final, the tower told us to "start your turn over the numbers", which we interpreted to mean to initiate the missed approach turn to 275 at the MAP instead of climbing to 700 ft before starting the turn. I assumed that the tower wanted to get us out of the way of the other traffic that wanted to land at BLI.

We executed the turn as instructed, expecting a subsequent instruction to contact Victoria Terminal on reporting execution of the missed approach, climbing and turning to 275. After a short period, we were told by the Tower to fly runway heading and we turned to 160, continuing the climb. I assumed that the tower was having us fly in a direction that would enable interception of the published missed course of 275, having achieved an offset to the west that provided separation for the landing traffic.

I was expecting a "hand off" to Victoria Terminal for the vectors that would get us back onto the published missed approach when the tower asked us if we wanted to continue or be handed back to Victoria Terminal. My student responded (incorrectly) that we wanted to return to ZZZ. Because we were still on an IFR clearance, he should have told the tower we wanted to be handed-off to Victoria Terminal.

The Tower then told us to turn "south east which will pass you across the extended centerline for runway 16" (a paraphrase). My student interpreted this to mean that we were cleared to proceed direct to ZZZ. I was still expecting the handoff to Terminal. The Tower then became concerned about our course, directed us to turn to 250, then 270, and to contact Victoria Terminal.

We had been climbing throughout these maneuvers on the way to 5,000 ft. I can't recall if the tower issued the altitude instruction or if Victoria Terminal made the assignment when we checked in; Terminal may have also made the assignment to 270.

Victoria Terminal asked if we had a moment "to talk". At that point we were stabilized in a climb to 5,000 on the assigned course of 270, effectively back on the missed approach.

Victoria Terminal asked us to explain what had just happened. I said that we'd been instructed to start our turn over the numbers, then had been issued vectors by the tower for traffic avoidance, and then were instructed to fly 250 (and I think 270, but that may have been the initial vector after contacting Victoria Terminal).

Victoria Terminal told us we had been instructed to fly the published missed approach and that the tower was listening to my explanation. VT subsequently said that we should have requested clarification when we received the vectors that modified its original instruction to fly the published missed approach. I agreed and apologized for any confusion on our part.

I was never told whether we had responded to instructions intended for or issued to other traffic or had misunderstood the vectors that had been issued to us. My student promptly read back all vectors that we thought were issued to our flight. We weren't corrected after any read back. I'd hoped to listen to a recording of the radio traffic on LiveATC.net to review what I thought we'd been told and determine how we might have misunderstood the vectors, but BLI traffic isn't recorded by this service.

Lessons Learned:

The major lesson learned for me is to request clarification or confirmation (even after a read back) for any instruction that modifies a missed approach procedure after initiating execution.

While we did not see the other traffic, I don't believe that there was a conflict. It seemed to me that the other traffic was behind us, in the course of receiving vectors to join the pattern as VFR traffic. The day was hazy with an overcast.

NOTES:

CONFUSED WHEN ISSUED A TURN BY ATC

ASRS, 2016

I was on a solo cross country to Austin TX. It was my first time flying solo into the Austin Class C (from which I departed the day before).

Conditions were marginal VFR the whole way. I used Foreflight for my weather briefing and waited for departure until all airports along my route indicated Marginal VFR or VFR. Visibility remained around 3 - 6 miles along the route.

For most of the route I stayed at 2,000 MSL to remain 500 below clouds (with no clearly visible could base). Marginal VFR is certainly somewhat stressful - added to the fact that it is a first solo into the Class C. I made contact with Austin Approach South around 25 miles from the Class C airspace, got my squawk code and confirmed radar contact.

Shortly after first making contact the controller alerted me that I had traffic approaching from my right (approaching from the east). He asked if I could climb to 2,500. Clouds in the Austin area were 3,000 or higher (although very hazy). I obliged.

I use a Stratus receiver and could see the traffic on my receiver. Sure enough, a few minutes later I saw the traffic (a low wing piston single) fly past about 1,000 below me. Kudos to the controller. I felt well cared for. I reported the traffic in sight. Some minutes later, the controller asked me to turn to 020, but he did not say the DIRECTION of turn. Had he said, "turn RIGHT to 020" I would not be writing this report. As it turned out, my heading indicator had drifted off quite a bit from the wet compass. I had flown most of the route using a basic auto pilot - simply adjusting the heading bug to keep my plane firmly on the track line on my Ipad (without paying much attention to the actual heading and variance from the wet compass).

I suddenly found myself in a somewhat stressful situation. The heading indicator did not line up with the wet compass and I had to make a heading adjustment as instructed by ATC. Instead of calmly getting this sorted out, I (wrongly) dubbed in that the controller is trying to get me out of harms way again and I turned 220 - heading west. The radio was very busy and I figured "he has me on radar and he must have good reason for getting me away from the airport." (In retrospect, all the controller wanted to do was set me up slightly east of the airport for a left hand downwind to runway 17 left).

After a few minutes the controller came back with something along the lines of, "You are heading west. Do you have a gyro problem? You are getting close to San Marcos airspace." We had a few exchanges back and forth and my mistake became apparent as I finally turned around to 020. The next instruction was "turn right 20 degrees". Easy to understand.

I soon found myself set up east of the airport and cleared to land on Runway 17 left. I heard another plane on the frequency saying that they have to overshoot their approach as "They were set up too high for the approach" or something along those lines. Once back on the tower frequency, that plane asked the controller if the Approach controller was in training. There was some exchange that implied he was.

I had very good situational awareness on my iPad as I approached the airport. As I said, if the word RIGHT was used I would have seen where he was going with this.

I dubbed in he had some traffic avoidance agenda and in my somewhat stressful state I just wanted to follow instructions without question.

A "we're setting you up to the east of the airport" may have helped.

For my part, I could have admitted that my heading indicator was off and that I was a little confused. Anyway, it all ended well and I know the controller did his best. He certainly kept me safe.

Lessons Learned:

I learned from it. I hope that the importance and value of simply adding the direction of turn with every heading indication given is stressed by this report.

NOTES:

ATC VS SAFETY

ASRS, 2018

Pilot departed on VFR flight to ZZZ under an ADIZ/FRZ flight plan I filed VFR as conditions were clearing and were forecasted to improve. As broken layers existed the Pilot (myself) requested ILS 23 approach from Approach [Control] and was granted flight following and given vectors. I was under impression I was IFR at this time as it was MVFR.

I was given vectors to the ILS 23 at ZZZ, and I was passed off to ZZZ Tower and proceeded on the ILS. A communication was made that was stepped on, I requested ZZZ Tower to say again. ZZZ Tower then asked if I was IFR or VFR. I assumed I was IFR and responded so.

On short final ZZZ Tower wanted me to discontinue the approach and exit the Class D airspace since he could not legally allow me to land in a MVFR field and wanted me to exit the airspace. I explained due to safety of flight I was not going to depart VFR into possible IFR due to PIC judgment of safety of flight I was unable to comply.

The legal conversation continued as I landed.

At this time I had a clear runway and was not in any layers and had a good glide path. I was not going to break off the approach and enter IFR conditions with passengers (possibly to be left to die flying VFR in IFR conditions, or possibly violate the ADIZ, before we reestablished) before I got picked back up by a possibly very busy Approach ATC dealing with commercial traffic, then air file a new IFR flight plan, re-establish a second approach and work back to where I already was due to the fields legal issue. All when I had a runway in sight and the flight was at that point safe and given excellent services.

Due to the safety of flight issue as PIC I did comply with ATC instructions. During the final I believe, after asking, I responded I was ok continuing under my own responsibility. With busy Approach [Controller] I have waited and orbited 20 minutes for my FRZ flight plan to be picked up in this region south of ZZZ.

Lessons Learned:

The Tower's legal requirements of a clearing weather condition forcing me back into an unknown weather condition did not mean more to me than the safe conduct of my flight and protection of my passengers under services. Other than this point, services were excellent and I complied as much as possible with ATC instructions. As I was under services up to final and had runway in sight I was not going to do a missed approach, be dropped from the airspace system, proceed without them into possible IFR and reestablish in the air, just to get back where I already was. I was given a [phone] number to call after I tied down and was informed that a M.O.R. (pilot deviation) was going forward. I was not given the FAA operator numbers of personnel involved after I requested it, just a supervisor number. This disadvantages me in the coming MOA process.

NOTES:

REQUESTING ASSISTANCE FROM
ATC IN IMC CONDITIONS

ASRS, 2018

I was flying from ZZZ to ZZZ1. When I was in the TRACON area, I flew through a cloud at 4,500 feet. I kept my wings level and flew my course line keeping an eye on my GPS and six pack. I ended up going through another cloud at 4,000 feet and another at 3,500 feet.

After informing TRACON every time I went through a cloud, TRACON asked if I would like to pick up an IFR flight plan. Not being instrumented rated, I informed him I was not personally Instrument Rated, but he kept offering for me to pick up a plan. I had only experienced clouds during the day during training. Experiencing night clouds were totally different and very freaky because of my lights in the cloud - without the lights though, it was only black (making the situation even scarier).

I asked after going through a third cloud to divert to ZZZ2. The controller started reading off vectors and mentioned a cloud of precipitation off the west side of ZZZ2. Turns out I was going through clouds that had randomly popped up with the rain. These clouds were not reported on the ATIS/AWOS.

Also, I was pointed towards a dark empty part of the terrain making it almost impossible to tell I was in a cloud until I was in one.

I decided to continue on at 3,000 feet because in order to divert I would have to fly through more clouds (the pop up rain) to get to ZZZ2. I continued on and the flight was otherwise uneventful.

Lessons Learned:

It was super nerve wracking going through clouds at night. I had never experienced it before.

I think it is important Private Pilots experience IFR conditions at night to remain calm like I had in these situations. I did everything to keep the plane level and descend down, but it was still scary since it was all new to me.

<u>NOTES:</u>

REQUESTED ATC ASSISTANCE DUE TO ICING

ASRS, 2014

I was working combined sectors. There was a lot of weather in the airspace, particularly low altitude IMC conditions. I had a LJ35 going to an airport without a functioning instrument approach that I was having to vector. I had a VFR at 6500 who was trying to get an IFR clearance, another that was at 6500 that I lost radar on, and an IFR clearance request through FSS. I took a handoff on [C172], VFR at 10000, level.

Shortly after she checked in, she said she was in IMC conditions and was looking for help. I didn't have anyone in that area and told her that I didn't know what the conditions were in that area. I asked her if she was qualified and capable of IFR flight; she said yes. I gave her an IFR clearance at 11000 (the altitude she was level at the time) and present heading because she was tracking on about a 100 heading or so. She acknowledged the clearance.

I saw her start to track more to the SE, which made me wonder what she was doing, although I assumed it was because she was in a turn that I missed due to the slow radar update.

Shortly after that she said she was in the middle of a storm and needed help. I had absolutely no NEXRAD depiction on the scope, at least not in that area. I asked her if she could climb to 12000, which she said yes to.

I had an IFR aircraft right above her at 13000 going east who I got a PIREP from. He said it was basically VMC at 13000, and that he was between layers, and that it was better back behind him.

I told the C172 about the traffic. She said she couldn't make 13000. I gave her additional vectors back to the west based on the information of the weather being better. I saw she was having trouble making 12000, so I gave her a block 11000 to 12000.

Subsequently she started accumulating ice and I did everything I could think of to get her to lower MEA areas. I suggested she go back [east] instead of trying to head [west], which she accepted.

I gave her the VOR frequency and TACAN channel for ZZZ VORTAC (she didn't have GPS). I gave her a new short range clearance and gave her the current weather observation. I gave her a descent to 8000, but she was still picking up ice.

I then lost her on radar, but had her report level at 8000 and reset her transponder, assuming her workload could support it. She reset the transponder, but she showed 300-400 feet low.... I gave her a 210 heading, gave her a descent to 6000, and turned her more westerly to get her lined up with final at ZZZ.

Just below 7000 she said she was in VMC. I asked her if the ice was flaking off the wings, she said yes.

Lessons Learned:

I told the FLM [of the assistance I gave] for her (after the first couple of problems), but that I never really told her because I didn't want her freaking out.

She was already scared enough.

As to the actual issue with the emergency and icing, there isn't much I can do to provide a recommendation on that.

However, the storm she reported being inside showed up on NEXRAD about 15 minutes after she ended up inside it.

Without more real time updates in NEXRAD, this kind of thing will continue to happen.

I can't guide aircraft to miss weather that isn't going to show up on the scope until 15 minutes after it shows up in the sky.

NOTES:

CHAPTER 8

NEAR MISS & SEPARATION

"I flew F-16's for the better part of a decade. The jet was designed in the late 60's and has aged better than almost any aircraft in the world. The one aircraft that beats it is the Cessna 172."

Major Justin "Hasard" Lee
    U.S. Air Force F-35 Fighter pilot

NEAR MIDAIR COLLISION
CESSNA 172

ASRS, 2018

Narrative: 1

I was with a student in a Cessna 172 on final. The student was flying. Passing approximately 400 feet, I saw off to our left, another Cessna 172 turning from base to our final approach path. We were close enough to read the tail number.

I told tower about this and that we were going around. Tower told that other 172 that they were explicitly instructed to follow behind us and land number two.

I took controls from my student and went around while performing an evasive turn to the right to avoid the other aircraft. We landed without incident.

My student and I discussed the importance of looking around, in particular at non-towered airports.

I had also been demonstrating the unique features of the GPS system in our aircraft that gives traffic alerts. It warned us successfully at the exact moment I spotted the aircraft.

Narrative: 2

Immediately preceding the incident, I was practicing landings and
take-offs for a stage check in my flight training at the end of this week.
I had 7-8 laps in the pattern with some varying instructions from
ATC due to larger aircraft in the area and departing the parallel
runway. More than once I received advice of wake turbulence and
one early crosswind turn due to a departing 737 on the parallel.

During the course of the training flight, I noticed I was hearing
clearances and instructions for runway XXL (my side of the pattern)
as well as XXR (the larger runway), apparently by the same
controller. I was intermittently hearing transmitting aircraft for XXR
(potentially wrong frequency, or perhaps as directed).

In any case, I was able to hear traffic for both runways on
frequency. On my intended final lap in the pattern, I was instructed
to extend downwind for spacing. I acknowledged and extended
downwind as directed. After I had extended downwind by some
distance, I called Tower and requested a full stop landing as I
intended to conclude the flight having satisfied my stated goal. I
noted that I had passed an aircraft landing on my downwind, on the
same runway, and mentally noted that this was likely the reason for
my extended downwind.

Immediately after calling tower with this request, I received the
following response for my tail number: "Aircraft Y Runway XXL
cleared to land". As this was not followed by an indication of
sequence (almost invariably "number 2, cleared to land"), I incorrectly
deduced that I could proceed to make my downwind turn.

At this point, I heard Aircraft Z, the aircraft behind me, communicating with Tower regarding position.

I didn't hear the full transmission, but it was apparent that there
was some confusion as to where Tower thought Aircraft Z was
located in the pattern.

As I turned final, I noticed Aircraft X on my right wing, to the west, a little close for comfort, but not to a degree that it caused immediate alarm as the runways are in very close proximity to each other; I often parallel other traffic on final at this particular airport. I believe the proximity was not as much of a concern as it should have been as the traffic typically approaching XXR is larger, thus skewing perspective slightly.

I had heard Aircraft X cleared for the visual approach, but due to radio noise, didn't have clarity as to which runway (left or right) had been specified. Based on position, I perceived it was possible that they were on approach to XXR. Again, no advice from ATC on spacing, sequence or otherwise. Just before I called Tower to ask what Aircraft X was doing or for further instruction, Aircraft X called Tower advised that they were executing an immediate go-around due to proximity to my aircraft.

Tower indicated that I should have been behind Aircraft X for landing, after Aircraft X announced their go-around intention, then confirmed a left pattern for landing for Aircraft X. After a standard landing, I was handed off to ground as normal.

After completing my checklists, contacting ground, and being cleared to taxi back to the ramp, I secured the airplane as usual.

Lessons Learned:

I should have confirmed the intentions of Aircraft X MUCH earlier in this case, or asked for confirmation to make my base turn.

Tower was fairly busy, as indicated by almost constant radio traffic for the preceding 10 minutes, but it was my mistake for not clarifying ATC instructions.

Aircraft X, which I believe was a student and an instructor, reacted appropriately and quickly once they realized we were flying the same approach. I attribute this partly to the fact that the instructor was exhibiting good situational awareness.

Additionally, they had the assurance that we were on approach to the same runway (as they were the aircraft on the right and I was aligned with the left-most runway; there's no chance I was on approach for the parallel). Additionally, hearing clearances for both runways further with frequent double transmissions added to confusion as to which runway was to be used.

I believe this was a case of ATC having a heavy workload (thus lack of clarity in landing clearance), and a lack of confirmation of instructions and delayed reaction on my part.

After landing and securing the aircraft on the ramp, the gravity of what could have happened was at the forefront of my mind, to the point that I became physically ill.

While I'm relieved that I didn't panic while still flying, this was still a situation that should not have happened and could have been avoided. I'm certain this lesson will stick with me for the rest of my flying experience.

<u>NOTES:</u>

CONTROLLED NEAR MIDAIR COLLISION

ASRS, 2019

Narrative: 1

I was flying as pilot in command from the right seat, with another pilot in the left seat. We were coming back from the local practice area after practicing Lazy 8's and were in ZZZ's Delta airspace by this point. After requesting to stay in the pattern for some performance landing practice, Tower asked us to switch frequency. This frequency is usually used when the Tower is busy and needs a separate frequency for traffic in the pattern.

We were instructed to make straight in for Runway XXL, and I complied. I was lined up on centerline on an extended final when Tower asked me if I was lined up for XXL. I told them I was. Looking back on this, I believe this may be because the traffic we nearly collided with was to our left and I assume they were cleared for XXR.

After Tower asked to clarify my position, I noticed on the G430W traffic display that traffic [was] very quickly approaching in a descent from above and our back left.

As the traffic gets closer to us I pull carburettor and throttle, descending to get out of the way. I asked Tower if they had the location of the traffic above us, and if they were speaking with this traffic. To my recollection all Tower had to say regarding my second question was something like, "No, they are not on my frequency." I assumed that meant the traffic was on the normal Tower frequency.

For about 30 seconds the traffic appeared to be exactly on top of us and at an altitude anywhere from zero to three hundred feet above us, continuing the descent with us.

After a brief level off of a couple of seconds to reassess where the traffic was and to consider the terrain below me, the other pilot told me to continue my descent because the traffic was still very close to us. The traffic passed off of our right side and lined up for XXR. They [were] only a couple of hundred feet from us to our 2 o'clock.

Once we had traffic in sight we discontinued the rate of our descent and initiated a go-around because of the un-stabilized approach we made. The other pilot landed the plane.

We decided to make the landing a full-stop and terminate the rest of the practice because we were shaken up.

Narrative: 2

Myself (Instrument Rated SEL Pilot) and the Pilot Flying (Commercial Rated SEL Pilot) were on approach to Runway XXL at ZZZ. The pilot flying was in the right seat and I was monitoring from the left seat. (Note this aircraft does not require 2 flight crewmembers, however, since we were both practicing maneuvers, 2 of us were there).

We were directed by Tower to tune to a separate frequency typically used for aircraft doing pattern work on Runway XXL. The Tower queried us on whether we were lined up for XXL, which we replied in the affirmative. Shortly after, I noticed another aircraft on our G430W traffic advisory system quickly approaching from approximately our 7 o'clock position.

This aircraft was initially indicating approximately 300 feet above our present altitude and descending. We queried the Tower whether or not they were talking to this aircraft, and the controller responded that she wasn't, but the controller on the main Tower frequency was, and apparently the traffic was landing on the parallel Runway XXR.

The traffic advisory showed our aircraft converging at approximately the same altitude, and we immediately took action to descend because this traffic was descending faster and was essentially on top of us.

The Mooney (we believe this was a Mooney) is a low wing aircraft, and the C172 is a high wing aircraft, making it exceptionally difficult to see one another. Eventually, after descending well below the glide slope on final, we saw the Mooney approximately 250 feet horizontally and 100 feet above us at our 2 o'clock position.

The pilot flying in our C172 continued the approach and performed a go-around maneuver due to our approach at this point being unstabilized. I then took over the aircraft and performed a normal pattern and approach to a full stop landing.

We decided to discontinue at that time due to being somewhat "shaken-up" over the incident.

Lessons Learned:

Narrative: 1

I am not sure how much I descended or how fast. I did not receive a terrain warning on my G430 but we were under the glide slope as indicated by the PAPI's.

Also of note, the traffic was a low wing airplane and we are a high wing, making it hard to see each other.

I believe the controller needed to do a better job verifying the other pilot was talking to Tower, and in initiating traffic-avoiding instructions to us both.

When Tower uses two separate frequencies for the parallel runways, it should be instructed [for] the pilots to monitor both.

Narrative: 2

I believe the controller we were talking to may have been relatively new and it was fairly busy on Local Control at the time, but either ourselves or the Mooney should have been given instructions to de-conflict the potential collision on the approach.

ZZZ Class Delta airspace can get relatively busy, and when the pattern frequency is separated, both controllers on Local need to coordinate to avoid conflicts such as this.

A phone call was made to the Tower explaining our encounter approximately 20 minutes after the event occurred.

NOTES:

MIDAIR COLLISION IN THE TRAFFIC PATTERN

ASRS, 2018

Narrative: 1

I was with a student in a Cessna 172 on final. The student was flying.

Passing approximately 400 feet, I saw off to our left, another Cessna 172 turning from base to our final approach path. We were close enough to read the tail number.

I told Tower about this and that we were going around. Tower told the other 172 that they were explicitly instructed to follow behind us and land number two.

I took controls from my student and went around while performing an evasive turn to the right to avoid the other aircraft.

We landed without incident.

Narrative: 2

Immediately preceding the incident, I was practicing landings and take-offs for a stage check in my flight training at the end of this week.

I had 7-8 laps in the pattern with some varying instructions from ATC due to larger aircraft in the area and departing the parallel runway. More than once I received advice of wake turbulence and one early crosswind turn due to a departing 737 on the parallel.

During the course of the training flight, I noticed I was hearing clearances and instructions for runway XXL (my side of the pattern) as well as XXR (the larger runway), apparently by the same controller. I was intermittently hearing transmitting aircraft for XXR (potentially wrong frequency, or perhaps as directed).

In any case, I was able to hear traffic for both runways on frequency. On my intended final lap in the pattern, I was instructed to extend downwind for spacing. I acknowledged and extended downwind as directed. After I had extended downwind by some distance, I called Tower and requested a full stop landing as I intended to conclude the flight having satisfied my stated goal. I noted that I had passed an aircraft landing on my downwind, on the same runway, and mentally noted that this was likely the reason for my extended downwind.

Immediately after calling tower with this request, I received the following response for my tail number: "Aircraft Y Runway XXL cleared to land". As this was not followed by an indication of sequence (almost invariably "number 2, cleared to land"), I incorrectly deduced that I could proceed to make my downwind turn.

At this point, I heard Aircraft Z, the aircraft behind me, communicating with Tower regarding position.

I didn't hear the full transmission, but it was apparent that there was some confusion as to where Tower thought Aircraft Z was located in the pattern. As I turned final, I noticed Aircraft X on my right wing, to the west, a little close for comfort, but not to a degree that it caused immediate alarm as the runways are in very close proximity to each other; I often parallel other traffic on final at this particular airport. I believe the proximity was not as much of a concern as it should have been as the traffic typically approaching XXR is larger, thus skewing perspective slightly.

I had heard Aircraft X cleared for the visual approach, but due to radio noise, didn't have clarity as to which runway (left or right) had been specified. Based on position, I perceived it was possible that they were on approach to XXR. Again, no advice from ATC on spacing, sequence, or otherwise. Just before I called Tower to ask what Aircraft X was doing or for further instruction, Aircraft X called Tower advised that they were executing an immediate go-around due to proximity to my aircraft.

Tower indicated that I should have been behind Aircraft X for landing, after Aircraft X announced their go-around intention, then confirmed a left pattern for landing for Aircraft X. After a standard landing, I was handed off to ground as normal.

After completing my checklists, contacting ground, and being cleared to taxi back to the ramp, I secured the airplane as usual.

Lessons Learned:

Narrative: 1

My student and I discussed the importance of looking around, in particular at non-towered airports.

I had also been demonstrating the unique features of the GPS system in our aircraft that gives traffic alerts. It warned us successfully at the exact moment I spotted the aircraft.

Narrative: 2

I should have confirmed the intentions of Aircraft X MUCH earlier in this case, or asked for confirmation to make my base turn. Tower was fairly busy, as indicated by almost constant radio traffic for the preceding 10 minutes, but it was my mistake for not clarifying ATC instructions.

Aircraft X, which I believe was a student and an instructor, reacted appropriately and quickly once they realized we were flying the same approach.

I attribute this partly to the fact that the instructor was exhibiting good situational awareness. Additionally, they had the assurance that we were on approach to the same runway (as they were the aircraft on the right and I was aligned with the left-most runway; there's no chance I was on approach for the parallel). Additionally, hearing clearances for both runways further with frequent double transmissions added to confusion as to which runway was to be used.

I believe this was a case of ATC having a heavy workload (thus lack of clarity in landing clearance), and a lack of confirmation of instructions and delayed reaction on my part.

After landing and securing the aircraft on the ramp, the gravity of what could have happened was at the forefront of my mind, to the point that I became physically ill. While I'm relieved that I didn't panic while still flying, this was still a situation that should not have happened and could have been avoided. I'm certain this lesson will stick with me for the rest of my flying experience.

<u>NOTES:</u>

A NEAR-MID-AIR-COLLISION

ASRS, 2014

Narrative: 1

I was flying in a training flight with my instructor. We were returning from pattern practice, and had been cleared by the tower official to do a touch-and-go.

On our final for the approach, another aircraft called in (SR20) and requested clearance for take-off. He was told to hold short of the runway and he did. Our aircraft (C172) had been cleared for takeoff, by Tower, from a touch-and-go and proceeded to depart the runway to stay in the pattern and come in for a final landing.

As we were climbing, the SR20 departed the runway approximately 10 seconds after we had started our initial climb. We turn crosswind and then downwind and maintained pattern altitude.

We had just finished the turn into downwind when we see to our left the SR20 wing high and banking for his crosswind to downwind turn all while at the same altitude as our aircraft. He was no more than 150 feet away from our aircraft.

My instructor immediately notified the Tower we were departing the pattern and took preventative action by first taking over control of the aircraft and then making a right 360 degree turn, as directed by the tower official. I stayed clear of all controls and let him maintain contact with the tower while manning the aircraft.

There was no sign of awareness of our aircraft indicated by the SR20.

The pilot did not make his presence known on the radio frequency.

Our aircraft is red and the sky was clear so we were visible in today's conditions. It appears he was not paying attention and decided on his own to make his crosswind to downwind turn far too soon.

We re-entered the pattern behind the other aircraft (per ATC instruction) and proceeded to follow additional tower instructions in regards to landing for a full stop and sequence instructions.

Narrative: 2

A student and I had flown inbound to ZZZ from the east to begin conducting pattern work. We were instructed to make a left base entry to Runway XX and were then cleared for the option on Runway XX, with an additional instruction to make left traffic after each option.

When we were on approximately a quarter mile final, a Cirrus, called the tower to request a departure clearance. The tower controller instructed the Cirrus to hold short for landing traffic -- my airplane. The Cirrus pilot read back the instruction and held short of the runway.

My student and I executed a touch-and-go landing on Runway XX and proceeded to climb on the upwind leg. Tower cleared the Cirrus for takeoff and instructed the pilot to make left traffic as well. While we were on upwind, I observed the Cirrus behind us and was aware of his position.

We turned left to join the crosswind leg for Runway XX. By this time we were already at pattern altitude. In a few seconds, we began the left turn to downwind. We were approximately halfway through this turn when I looked to the left and observed a Cirrus ahead and to my left, in a wing-high left bank, also joining the downwind leg at our same altitude. The Cirrus could not have been more than 150 feet away from us.

I took the controls from my student and immediately executed a right turn to the east and advised the tower that I was doing so as a result of being cut off on the downwind leg. Upon completion of a right 360 degree turn to rejoin the downwind as we were subsequently instructed, I had a chance to mentally assess the situation and realize how close we were to the Cirrus.

The tower cleared us to land, number 2 following the Cirrus we had just evaded. I made a full stop landing and taxied to the ramp without further incident. Once we were on the ground, I contacted the tower via phone to report an NMAC.

Narrative: 3

I was operating a Cirrus SR20 with my private pilot student who was learning takeoffs and landings at that time. During the initial climb after takeoff, we cut off a Cessna during the crosswind to downwind turn in the pattern.

My student was the pilot flying and he was learning pattern work at that time. In the previous lesson, I taught him the normal pattern procedure was to turn crosswind 300 feet below the pattern altitude after the initial climb if there is no other traffic.

Our Cirrus climbed faster than the Cessna in front of us, so we were at pattern altitude very quickly after takeoff, and my student started the crosswind turn before the preceding Cessna started the turn.

I believe that my student was busy trying to turn crosswind at 300 feet below pattern altitude, without noticing that the other Cessna traffic was still in the pattern. The Cessna made a right 360 degree turn to space up after he saw us, and we were cleared of conflict.

Lessons Learned:

Narrative: 2

I have been flying at this airport for several years and have been cut off in the pattern from time to time. That said, I have never experienced anything this close here, nor in 7 years of flying general aviation aircraft.

The Cirrus pilot lacked situational awareness and basic airmanship. The pilot was at the runway hold short line, presumably monitoring the tower frequency, when we were cleared for the option and were instructed to make left traffic thereafter.

When the pilot called the tower ready for departure, the pilot was instructed to hold short for landing traffic — my airplane. The Cirrus pilot was cleared for takeoff as soon as my aircraft's wheels left the ground approximately 3/4ths of the way down the runway.

My aircraft was red with white stripes — not exactly difficult to see during today's clear sky conditions. The pilot should have applied common sense.

A C-172 will climb slower than a Cirrus SR20.

Furthermore, this pilot should have been able to observe my aircraft turning from upwind to crosswind, or should have queried the tower as to my position had he lost sight of my airplane, regardless of whether or not he knew we would be remaining in the pattern.

I doubt the pilot had us in sight at all after we climbed beyond the departure end of the runway.

Narrative: 3

This happened due to our mistake. We should have stayed on upwind and wait for the Cessna to turn first, in order to prevent this from happening.

In the future, I would tell my student to always watch out for other traffic. If there's no other traffic, then it's okay to start the crosswind turn. However, if there's other traffic in front of us, make sure we follow the traffic first.

It's important to exercise extreme caution in the pattern and we will do our best to stay safe in the future.

NOTES:

AIRBORNE CONFLICT - CESSNA VS P51 MUSTANG

ASRS, 2017

In regards to the TCAS, I saw the plane on ForeFlight and my Garmin 430W ADS-B, which helped, though I did not know where the plane was going to go next.

I am an instrument rated private pilot with 220 hours of flight time (45 hours in the past 12 months), and I regularly fly up and down the coast as I am a member/director of a club with three airplanes.

I was operating a Cessna 172-R on a VFR flight to ZZZ with a stop at ZZZ1 for fuel. I departed at XA:42. Most, if not all, weather stations were reporting clear skies and unrestricted visibility along the entire route, so there was no need for an IFR flight plan. I was in contact with ATC for VFR flight following during the entirety of my flight. As expected, there were a lot of VFR pilots flying around the area due to the great weather.

Shortly before XB:00, I was cautioned by Approach of traffic circling up ahead. I knew of a plane event going on at ZZZ all weekend, so this was not totally unexpected.

I was notified by the Approach controller that she was not in contact with the plane. She later checked to see if the plane was in contact with ZZZ tower at the time, and was notified by the ZZZ tower controller that he was not. I maintained visual contact with the aircraft at all times as it made multiple 360 degree turns and climbed and descended thousands of feet at speeds almost doubling my ground speed.

As the controller was not in contact with the aircraft, I took evasive action (45 degree right turn) at XA:57 in an attempt to pass to the left side of (and behind). I then turned back towards the ocean in order to monitor what their next move would be.

The aircraft made a quick turn back to the southwest, and was headed directly for me from behind my tail. During this time, I was cautioned by the approach controller that the traffic was less than one mile at my five o'clock position and converging and at a speed of 100 knots faster than my ground speed (roughly 110 kts).

I made a left 360 degree turn (second instance of evasive action) at this time in order to avoid and did so with very little separation. I believe this is where my path crossed closest.

The aircraft unexpectedly headed back towards the ocean at this point, so I turned 30 to 45 degrees left (third instance of evasive action) to be further out towards the ocean. It appeared it headed back to ZZZ at this time and was out pacing me by 100 knots, so I headed back to ZZZ and was handed over to the tower by the Approach controller. While on the tower frequency, I heard the aircraft communicating with the tower which evidenced them having a functional two-way radio onboard. I landed without incident a few minutes later.

After parking and securing my airplane, I walked over the where the aircraft was parked and asked to speak to the pilot. I explained to him that I was in the area while he was conducting fast 360 degree turns and ascents and descents while the Approach controller was not in contact with him.

I also advised that I took evasive action three times due to the unpredictable nature of his flying and inability to communicate with him. He seemed to think my concerns were unreasonable and said that this was the seventh such flight that he conducted on this day.

He said, "We picked an area between two airways [to conduct these flights]." Looking at the chart, these appear to be an area which is heavily traveled by VFR pilots flying up and down the coast. As previously stated, the sky was clear with no visibility restrictions in the entire region.

I explained that I think for the safety of him, his paying passengers, and other pilots flying in the area like myself, he should obtain VFR flight following and advise the controllers of his intentions. He said, "We never talk to Approach."

I explained that while I understand he legally is not required to be talking to anyone in that region, it is in everyone's best interest for him to do so. He shrugged this off and it was clear that his behavior is not going to change going forward on this tour.

I asked him if he ever saw me during the flight, to which his response was, "I have TCAS." He did not acknowledge whether or not he saw me either via visual contact or via TCAS/ADS-B. The plane I was flying was equipped with ADS-B In/Out and his plane is at least equipped with ADS-B out as I saw the plane with its tail number on ForeFlight and the Garmin 430W.

I told the pilot that he was looping around me at almost double my speed, with the closest moment coming when he was approaching me from behind, and he said something to the effect of "If it's from behind why does it matter?" I proceeded to explain that he was traveling over 100 knots faster than me, to which he was silent. I left him with another recommendation to contact Approach for flight following to prevent from this happening to any other VFR pilots.

To me, the actions of this pilot display a careless and reckless operation of aircraft and disregard for the safety of his passengers, other pilots, other aircraft, and the aviation community as a whole, in violation of 14 CFR 91.13(a).

Despite my multiple instances of evasive action, and with the assistance of a very helpful Approach controller, I had multiple close calls attempting to avoid him.

At times, it felt as though I was helpless due to the speed of his aircraft and the unpredictability of where it would go next. It was the closest I have come to another plane in my nine years of flying experience. If nothing is done to remedy this situation, I believe that the pilot's behavior will not change and the nature of his flying and lack of communication is so reckless and negligent that the chances of a fatal accident are reasonably possible.

Lessons Learned:

From the conversation I had with the pilot, he seemed very lackadaisical about the entire event and its implications for the safety and well-being of others and it does not seem that his behaviors are going to change going forward.

A simple check in with Approach would have resulted in the controller being able to keep myself and the aircraft separated with ease. I am willing to cooperate in any investigation to the best of my ability.

<u>NOTES:</u>

UAV NEAR MISS

ASRS, 2018

I was with a student pilot and we were practicing full stop taxi-back landings at IWA. We were established about one mile west of the airport in left downwind for runway 30 Left.

Once approximately midfield, the local controller gave us instructions to make a right 360 in the downwind for sequencing with other traffic ahead. My student then read back the instructions and established us in a standard rate turn to the right. Both my student, who was pilot flying in the left seat and myself were looking outside for traffic when about 270 degrees into the right turn we both noticed a small object below the right wing at approximately our 2-o'clock position moving left to right.

Initially, I thought it was a small helicopter at a lower altitude but shortly after I observed a very bright flashing blue light atop a small black aircraft. Due to the size of the aircraft and the bright blue light on top, I concluded that it was a remote controlled drone.

After my student and I both saw this object, he continued his rollout to re-establish himself in the downwind for runway 30 left.

The object appeared to be hovering in very close proximity to us in the traffic pattern at an altitude that would have easily risked a collision for local traffic pattern operations.

Luckily, we did not have to take evasive action judging by the drone's slightly lower altitude but initially it caught us off guard.

I reported the sighting immediately to the local controller and estimated to him that the object was about 300 feet below us.

Following the flight, and subsequent debrief, both my student and I concluded that the object was very easy to see and that it could not have been more than 100 feet lower than our downwind altitude of 2600 feet MSL.

After this incident, the flight continued with no further issues. At the conclusion of our flight, another student at our flight school told me he also saw the object around the same time we reported our sighting to the control tower.

I am unsure if he has filed a report or what his position was at that time.

Lessons Learned:

I'm really not sure what could have been done to avoid this specific incident except to make the public more aware of flying drones in close proximity to airports, traffic patterns, and approach corridors as well as develop regulations for drone pilots regarding proximity of their fight operations near airports.

NOTES:

UNAWARE OF A NEAR MIDAIR COLLISION

ASRS, 2019

Pilot of C172:

I experienced a near midair collision in the vicinity of Byron Airport (C83) in Byron, California.

I was operating a C172 in the right closed traffic pattern for runway 30. I was with a student practicing landings in the traffic pattern. We were making regular position reports on the common traffic advisory frequency (CTAF) of 123.05. At the time, there were a significant amount of air traffic in the vicinity, including glider towing and parachute operations. The CTAF was noticeably congested, particularly with traffic calls from other airports.

While I was on right downwind to runway 30, I was aware there was 1 other airplane in the traffic pattern ahead of me, because I had heard their radio calls and could visually see them.

At some time, Aircraft Y reported they were on a right base to runway 30.

Almost immediately, another aircraft (whose tail number I cannot remember) responded on the CTAF by saying that they were also on right base to runway 30 and asked for Aircraft Y's specific location. I cannot remember the response on the CTAF.

At the same time, I did not see a second aircraft on the base leg. A few moments later, I made a radio call announcing that I was on right downwind for runway 30, and almost immediately Aircraft Y responded by announcing that they were also on right downwind for runway 30.

I was confused because I was sure I heard that aircraft call on base just a few moments ago. I pitched the nose down to initiate my descent, and visually saw Aircraft Y directly underneath my aircraft approximately 200 feet below and slightly ahead. I immediately took evasive action. I stopped the descent and navigated my airplane outside of Aircraft Y's flight path to the runway.

I was operating at 1100 feet MSL (mean sea level), and promptly stopped my descent, while keeping the aircraft in sight. I maneuvered away from the other aircraft to allow adequate separation before coming in for my landing.

During the entire approach, I was able to keep the aircraft in sight. After the landing, I made a full stop and taxi back where I tried to get the full registration of the aircraft. My student told me the registration, but I could not confirm this. The aircraft was using call sign "Aircraft Y" on the CTAF, which I heard myself. The airplane appeared to be a low-wing, single engine propeller plane. The airplane was last seen taxiing to the hangar area at Byron airport, where I elected not to follow them.

At the time of the incident, weather was VFR with generally good visibility and ceilings. I had obtained the weather at Byron prior to entering the traffic pattern. Winds were calm.

Lessons Learned:

Pilot of C172:

I believe the cause of the incident was Aircraft Y's decision to operate at an altitude below the TPA of 1,000 ft (traffic pattern altitude) above airport elevation. Additionally, I believe that Aircraft Y's radio call that they were on base was not accurate and led to confusion about the aircraft's actual position.

Pilot of Aircraft Y:

I was not aware there was a problem until contacted 5 days later I was landing at Byron airport CA (C83). As usual I announced 45 degree to 30 followed by downwind call, base call, final call and clear of runway 30 to taxi. I did hear and monitor other aircraft in the vicinity however no one announced they were in a downwind for 30. I was not informed on the radio before or after said incident nor did anyone inform me at anytime on the radio. I have not been told were he was relative to me so I don't know what the right of way criteria was.

<u>NOTES</u>:

TOO CLOSE FOR COMFORT

ASRS, 2018

I had taken off for closed traffic to practice some touch and go's. Weather conditions during this day were VFR with crosswinds, and aloft there was noticeable wind shear and quite a bit of turbulence. Surface winds were approximately 270 at 10G16 knots, the winds in the pattern at 1,000 feet were varying between 18 and 26 knots with approximately the same heading as the surface winds, as indicated by the Garmin G1000 avionics in the cockpit.

I made a radio call to report midfield downwind, and ATC indicated that I was number 2 to land following TBM on 6 mile final. ATC referenced the traffic at my 11 o'clock.

As I passed the runway threshold on downwind, I had visual identification of the aircraft in the distance and determined that at the time, it provided safe separation. I set my crab angle appropriately during downwind such that it provided a ground track that paralleled the runway and I maintained this heading throughout the episode.

As I prepared for the landing phase of the flight, I momentarily scanned inside the aircraft to monitor the instruments, and setup the aircraft appropriately for landing, and returned my gaze outside. However, the wind shear and turbulence were significant enough that I had to allocate much of my attention to maintaining a safe, straight and level position for several moments, and temporarily lost visual contact of the TBM.

I returned my attention to the distance to re-locate the TBM aircraft, however, at this point, the aircraft was at my 11 o'clock, 200 feet below (as I was told on the ground by ATC after I later landed). I am not sure of the horizontal separation, though it was too close for comfort. We were several miles away from the airport at this instance.

The TBM and I both maneuvered to briefly modify our course to ensure separation, and I remember briefly deviating right as he passed below and left of me, as I had been taught in flight training.

After passing the inbound traffic, the Tower asked if I had identified the TBM or if it may have been the Piper Arrow, which landed ahead of the TBM, and I confirmed that I believed it was indeed the TBM.

At this point in time, I glanced out the rear window of the Cessna 172, and noticed that the ground track had deviated inwards toward the approach corridor. I had not encroached on the runway heading, but had caused a deviation from my initially set downwind heading such that it appeared the wind had blown me inwards toward the approach corridor.

Lessons Learned:

My analysis of the situation, is that there was never a moment of imminent safety concern (as our respective aircraft remained several hundred feet away from each other and we both regained visual contact ahead of time), however, there was a moment that was too close for comfort and is worthy of debriefing.

The weather conditions during this day took my attention off of the inbound traffic at the wrong moment in time, and caused me to focus my attention on safely flying the airplane in challenging conditions.

As I had set my crab angle based off of what provided a parallel course to the runway on downwind, I imagine that the wind shear and crosswind gust may have changed sufficiently to cause the ground track to deviate left of the downwind course as I was maneuvering at this time in unstable air. I did not cross the runway track as I was able to visually ascertain through the rear window of the C172, however this was enough to push my ground track within a distance that was too close for comfort of the inbound aircraft.

I do not believe there was any negligence involved, although in hindsight, it does appear that a more generous or more divergent crab angle from the runway would have provided an extra factor of safety by over-correcting for the crosswind, and would have avoided the potential for any incident to occur.

I don't believe the TBM had visual contact of me until the two aircraft were too close for comfort, and after my initial identification of the traffic, my attention was taken away from the visual contact of the TBM and therefore provided the opportunity for convergence of the two aircraft.

As stated, I do not believe there was any imminent danger in this situation.

NOTES:

HARD LANDING AND RUNWAY EXCURSION

ASRS, 2015

As I entered the left downwind for Runway 35 at JYO I spotted a helicopter at the downwind to base leg of the pattern. I had not heard this aircraft make any calls. I inquired about what his intentions were, as he didn't appear to be following the conventional pattern to land. He said that he was landing, and would "only be on the ground for a minute". From this I assumed he was doing a touch and go.

I proceeded to extend my downwind to allow him more time to maneuver. I could only extend my downwind slightly, however, to avoid incurring the Special Flight Rules Area (SFRA). As I turned base, the helicopter was on the ground and I mentally prepared to go around if he wasn't able to take off in time.

At this time, Airport Operations came on the CTAF and advised that the helicopter was displacing debris and that a runway inspection was necessary. I announced my intention too, and then proceeded to turn from base to upwind and returned to traffic pattern altitude.

I was unable to spot the helicopter until I had reached the end of the runway on the upwind, where I had to call to find his position.

As I turned crosswind to downwind, the helicopter announced he would hover over the quarry nearby the airport to allow me and the other aircraft in the pattern to land.

The pattern was then uneventful until I was on short final. I was a bit shallow and slow, so I added power to ensure I got over the runway, then cut power. I rounded out uneventfully, however as I began to flare, a gust came across the runway at about 30 degrees to the runway, and shifted almost directly crosswind.

I had difficulty maintaining longitudinal alignment with the centerline and ended up with my nose at 45 degrees to the center-line. I misjudged my altitude over the runway, and pulled back hard on the yoke.

About two seconds later, I landed hard on both mains simultane-ously. I was still severely angled with respect to the centerline of the runway, however I was afraid of rolling the plane if I attempted to turn too rapidly.

I ran off the runway into the grass alongside the runway, avoiding runway lighting and signs along the runway, and reentered the runway within 20 seconds of leaving it. The aircraft behind me in the pattern went around uneventfully. There was no damage done to me or the aircraft.

Lessons Learned:

I believe that the combination of aircraft acting erratically in the pattern and Airport Operations inspecting the runway caused my normal flow of operations to be disrupted, and this led me to make mistakes on my landing.

<u>NOTES:</u>

WAKE VORTEX ENCOUNTER AND
FIRM LANDING

ASRS, 2015

I was performing a 1-hour Cessna 172 discovery flight for a potential Private Pilot student. The flight originated from ZZZ, and the incident occurred while landing back at ZZZ.

While in the traffic pattern maneuvering to land, the hour-meter rolled over to the pre-paid allocated flight time, allowing only one attempt at landing without overcharging the customer.

My aircraft was in landing configuration on short final. What I believed to be an EC130 helicopter had just completed his approach to the runway and was hovering on the runway centerline, near the 1000-foot aiming markers, as I best recall.

I communicated with the pilot of the helicopter via the CTAF, asking his intentions. The helicopter pilot promptly responded, stating that he was beginning his takeoff, and immediately began accelerating from a hover.

At this point, I believe I was arriving at the threshold and began my roundout/flare on the presumption that he would be clear of the runway, providing enough separation to complete my short-field landing. However, lateral separation was less than safely desirable.

In the unlikely event that the helicopter would have to abort his takeoff or I would have to commence a late go-around, my aircraft was not in a favorable position for collision avoidance. Additionally, the distraction of attempting to maintain separation from the helicopter led to a firm landing, resulting in an uncomfortable bounce.

Downwash from the helicopter may have played a factor as well.

I maintained positive control of the aircraft, completed the landing, and terminated the flight without incident to either aircraft.

Lessons Learned:

It is very evident that rather than attempt to land behind the departing traffic, I should have aborted the approach and made a second attempt. This would have resulted in paying more money than expected, but money should *never* be an excuse to compromise safety.

Had the helicopter pilot delayed his departure another second, I would have definitely aborted my landing. This is a prime example of external pressures leading to overconfidence and ultimately pushing the limits of my experience. Fortunately, only embarrassment resulted from this incident, and I am able to learn from my less-than-ideal decision.

NOTES:

CHAPTER 9

ENGINE CHALLENGES

"I landed! I landed! I landed! We're on the highway! We're on the highway!"

Richard Lee
    Flight instructor emergency landing a 172 on a South Florida highway June 11, 2021.

AN EMERGENCY IS DECLARED

ASRS, 2014

Narrative: 1

This Cessna 172S had just flown between seven and eight hours without anomaly. I was the front right passenger. I was handling radios and navigation for the PIC.

We landed with approximately 12-15 gallons of fuel. 5 gallons per side was added by the FBO. 100LL was requested. Neither myself nor the PIC watched the fueling of the aircraft. Prior to engine start, the PIC sumped all of the fuel drains and found no contamination. As part of the preflight activity a runup was accomplished nothing no anomaly.

We departed [after dark] and while climbing through 2,100 msl or so the engine experienced a severe hesitation. After determining that it was not pilot induced and remedies such as mixture/throttle adjustment would not cure the now rough engine an immediate left turn was made and an emergency was declared.

The controller acknowledged and offered a vector to the ILS and I declined, opting for a visual approach now that we had descended below the overcast. The only runway lights that came into view were those of runway XX (closed) on which we landed uneventfully. The engine (prop) stopped turning as we rolled to a stop.

At the point we rolled to a stop we both noticed that we had rolled onto an active runway. We immediately exited the aircraft and pushed it off of Runway and onto a taxiway where we were met by fire/rescue personnel.

Narrative: 2

Through a timeframe beginning around noon until shortly before the event I personally flew this aircraft on a crew ferry mission. The airplane traveled [on the first leg] with no abnormalities and took on 20 gallons of fuel. After the fuel was checked the aircraft departed on an IFR flight plan to (ZZZ). This leg was also flown with no abnormalities.

We purchased 10 gallons of gas from [the ZZZ FBO], bringing our onboard total to roughly 18 gallons. The fuel was checked and no contamination was noticed. We entered the aircraft for the last leg of the mission, and received clearance for our IFR flight. I was the pilot flying and Mr. X was working navigation and communications.

The aircraft performed engine start, taxi, and run-up with no abnormalities. After a brief delay we received clearance for takeoff and began talking with Approach on climb out. We entered into the overcast layer at 1900 FT, and upon reaching roughly 2100 FT-2200 FT the engine sputtered and experienced a loss of power.

Having my right hand already on the throttle I ensured that both it and the mixture were full open and rich, respectively. I ensured the fuel selector was set to "Both" and that the fuel shutoff valve was open. I then activated the electric auxiliary fuel pump.

Noticing persisting engine roughness and decreased power, I initiated a descending left turn to both exit the overcast layer and begin heading back. Simultaneously Mr. X declared an emergency and declined vectors to the ILS, as we had cleared the cloud deck. Searching for a suitable runway I flew a descending arc towards the airport, with the aircraft appearing to make less than normal power given the full-open position of the throttle. As we orbited the airfield from the 090 radial north-westward there was minor confusion to our exact location. Upon seeing definitive runway edge lights I chose to land the aircraft on that surface. It was unknown at the time what our selected runway was. The engine ceased to make power on the landing flare and the prop stopped windmilling on the ground roll. The aircraft came to rest just inside the edge of an active runway.

We quickly egressed the aircraft and pushed it off the runway and into a taxiway intersection. Seconds later we were met by emergency response personnel.

Lessons Learned:

Fuel management is critical to flight safety. Always keep an eye on fuel levels and monitor the fueling process to ensure the correct amount and type of fuel is added to the aircraft.

If an engine problem arises, prioritize safety by immediately declaring an emergency and taking appropriate action. Consider all available options for landing safely, including visual approaches and alternate landing sites.

Maintain situational awareness at all times during flight, including knowing the location of active runways and taxiways, and be prepared to take action to avoid potential hazards.

When in doubt, seek assistance from air traffic control or other resources available to you.

NOTES:

TRAINING WITH PARTIAL ENGINE FAILURE

ASRS, 2018

Narrative: 1

The event began as a training flight. The intended flight was to be a dual VFR cross country from ZZZ using pilotage and dead reckoning to ZZZ1, then GPS navigation from ZZZ1 to ZZZ2 and then ZZZ2 back to ZZZ. We completed a thorough run-up at ZZZ, with no engine issues. Takeoff, climb, and cruise to ZZZ1 was normal. After a full stop and taxi back, we continued to ZZZ2. During the cruise, I noticed that the number four CHT was a few bars higher than the rest of the cylinders. I inquired my instructor about it, and he believed it was nothing to worry about, since the number four cylinder is usually the hottest of all the cylinders.

Landing was normal at ZZZ2, and we stopped at the FBO for approximately forty-five minutes. My instructor and I completed an engine run-up, and there were no abnormal indications. We then took off on runway XXL, and I noticed the engine seemed to be making a deeper and somewhat louder noise than usual.

Once we began the after-takeoff checklist, my instructor checked the CHTs and noticed that the number four CHT was at 515 degrees and rising (normal operating range for the C172 being 200 - 500 degrees, and [guidance] calling for no more than 400 degrees). We immediately contacted tower and informed them that we needed to land back on runway XXL due to an engine issue. They asked my instructor if we wanted to declare an emergency, and he elected to not, since we did not have any other abnormal conditions. During the precautionary landing, my instructor noticed the number four CHT reach over 550 degrees. Upon landing, we taxied back to the FBO and informed [the rental FBO] about the situation.

A mechanic from [a nearby field] was contacted and he tested the CHT temperature probes and was unable to find anything definite due to not having the necessary tools. Afterwards, a mechanic and another flight instructor flew in a PA-44 from [ZZZ] to attempt to fix the engine. The mechanic performed multiple tests throughout the day and was unable to fix the problem. He discussed the problem with his superiors and they all had strong reason to believe that the issue was a faulty temperature probe. We all ended up staying overnight in ZZZ2 since neither instructor was night-current in the PA-44.

In the morning, the mechanic conducted several more tests and my instructor explained to me that the mechanic found that some of the protective wiring on one of the wires was frayed, so he wrapped it in electrical tape and it seemed to stabilize the number four CHT from rising as much during the tests. After contacting several personal, we all believed that the aircraft was safe to fly and began to brief for takeoff.

My instructor and I were advised to keep the mixture full rich during the entire flight to assist in CHT cooling in the small chance that the issue was not a faulty CHT probe. We planned to increase all speeds of the takeoff and climb as well to ensure optimal engine cooling.

The mechanic explained to us that we should monitor the EGT and use that as our reference instead of the CHT since the issue was likely the faulty CHT probe. We then discussed what airports we could use in the event of an emergency along the route and found that there were a significant number available for the majority of the trip. We then conducted an engine run-up and did not notice any anomalies.

We then took off on runway XY and again noticed the CHT climbing, but the EGT remained normal. I rotated at 63 KIAS (55 KIAS was what [guidance] called for), initially climbed at 85 KIAS (we normally used 74 KIAS for this phase), and then cruise climbed at 90 KIAS [FBO] normally uses 85 KIAS for this), and kept the mixture full rich the entire flight; thus, we were taking multiple precautions to avoid an engine overheat.

During the climb, I noticed the same seemingly louder and deeper engine noise but continued flying since we were told that the issue should be the CHT probe, and not a cylinder issue. The CHT rose again to over 500 degrees, but the EGT was reading normal. We initially planned to fly 2500 MSL and then to 6500 MSL but stayed at 3000 MSL due to some scattered clouds.

Once we were cruising, the engine noise slowly grew louder and more noticeable. We then were about to climb to 3500 MSL, approximately fifteen to twenty minutes into the flight, I noticed a significantly louder noise from the engine, somewhat like a deep, metallic clanging noise. I informed my instructor, and immediately he also noticed the engine was vibrating substantially.

We realized that we were having hazardous engine trouble and [notified ATC].

Until this point, I had been the pilot flying. I gave the controls to my instructor and he began coordinating with ATC the nearest airport, what heading to fly, and answered the standard emergency questions. We received a heading to ZZZ3, and my instructor increased the throttle to full power in an attempt to gain as much power as possible.

We only had approximately 2100 RPM (C172 normally provides 2700 RPM at full power), and the RPM was slowly decreasing. I then noticed that the EGT had massively spiked on the number four cylinder, and it was reading over 1460 degrees.

My instructor kept us between 3000 and 3200 feet MSL until we were within a few miles of the airport and made an emergency descent to ZZZ3. The CHT had cooled during the descent due to the increased airflow, but the engine was still violently vibrating and the number four EGT was still massively higher than the other cylinders. We side-slipped down to runway YY and landed without incident. We had the PA-44 with the mechanic follow us out of ZZZ2 in the case of an emergency, so they landed shortly thereafter and inspected the engine. The mechanic immediately noticed a large crack around the number four cylinder, oil splattered across the lower cowling and several exhaust pipes, and a burn mark behind the number four cylinder.

Narrative: 2

I was conducting a cross-country with my student. We landed at ZZZ1, taxied back to the active runway and proceeded directly to ZZZ2. After reaching cruise altitude to ZZZ2, my student and I noticed the CHT of the #4 Cylinder was indicating hotter than the other three. The #4 cylinder was stable and within limitations.

We landed at ZZZ2, refuelled, and filed [our flight plan]. We then taxied to runway XXL at ZZZ2, completed the run-up and all engine indications were normal and within limitations. The #4 CHT was still indicating hotter than the other three cylinders. After being cleared to take-off runway XXL, we were about 600 feet AGL, at 85 KIAS (to keep the CHT cool).

I checked the CHTs on the MFD and the #4 Cylinder was flashing red. We had a positive exchange of flight controls and I was flying the aircraft immediately after this occurred.

I immediately contacted tower and requested to return back to land. I was then cleared to enter the left downwind for runway XXL and cleared to land.

After landing we shut the aircraft down at [the FBO] and I contacted [the rental FBO] management and maintenance. Maintenance contacted a nearby aircraft mechanic. The aircraft mechanic could not find a solution to the #4 high-temperature indication. [They] flew an instructor in a Piper Seminole and one aircraft mechanic to work on the aircraft. The mechanic could not find the solution to the #4 Cylinder high-temperature indication.

We stayed the night because it was getting very late at night and the instructor who flew the Seminole was not night current to carry passengers. After spending the night at a hotel, we arrived at the [FBO] at ZZZ2, preflighted the Seminole to return back to ZZZ. The Seminole instructor filed an IFR flight plan back to ZZZ.

After taxiing out and holding short behind [another aircraft] at runway XC, I received a call from the [Operations Director]. He requested that we cancel the takeoff and taxi back to the airplane because [he] wants our A&P Mechanic to conduct more tests on aircraft.

After arriving back to [the FBO] support, the A&P mechanic conducted more tests but was still unable to lower the #4 CHT indication. The A&P mechanic completed one last test and was able to lower the #4 CHT to the normal operating range. After the A&P mechanic discussed the situation with [the rental FBO], and they concluded that the aircraft is airworthy. Based on the previous tests and the competent advice from the maintenance department, they all came to the consensus that the aircraft was safe to fly. I agreed with their decision and the A&P signed and dated all previous maintenance discrepancies.

My student and I conducted a normal preflight of the aircraft, completed a normal run-up and the A&P mechanic was able to see the #4 CHT temperature gauge from the outside.

The A&P mechanic walked around and checked while my student and I were in the aircraft on the ramp.

He gave us the thumbs up and I agreed because all engine indications (i.e. EGT and CHT indications) were within normal operating ranges and stable. During the taxi out to the active runway XY at ZZZ2, I was closely monitoring the #4 CHT indication and EGT indication as well. All indications were in the normal operating range. I did one more close check of the CHT and EGT before the taxiing onto the runway, and I saw all engine indications were in the normal operating range before advancing the throttles. The A&P mechanic told us that we need to have the mixture rich during the whole entire flight to aid in cooling the CHT.

After taking off of runway XY at ZZZ2, I had my student rotate at 55 KIAS (flaps up Vr) and climb out at 90 KIAS cruise climb to help keep the CHTs cool. After levelling off at 3000 feet before a 4000 scattered cloud layer, I told Departure that I cannot climb to the assigned 6500 cruising altitude back to ZZZ. We were cleared at or below 3500 feet until we were able to do our VFR climb to 6500 feet. About 10-15 minutes after departure from ZZZ and around 2900-3100 feet, my student and I were told to contact Approach.

After contacting Approach, my student and I were monitoring the CHT and EGTs and we both saw a rising EGT temperature on the #4 cylinder, but the CHT was not rising... We both heard a strange noise from the engine, felt a shaking sensation, and saw the engine cowling shaking as well. Immediately after this, the EGT indication rose rapidly to 1460 degrees. I immediately heard and felt engine roughness and a decrease in engine RPM.

I immediately contacted Approach and notified them of the situation. I told the controller that I needed vectors to the closest airport and distance. The controller told me to turn to a heading of 180. I turned to the heading of 180 and saw [another] airport (ZZZ3) in front of me. I told my student to run the checklist while I fly the airplane and communicate with ATC.

The controller during the whole entire time was very professional and calm. The controller wanted us to write down a frequency and number to contact them when we landed. I told my student to write the number and frequency down, which he did. I saw runway YY insight at ZZZ3 airport and knew I was going to make the runway.

We experience the engine failure/roughness around 7-8 miles North East of ZZZ3 airport around 3100 feet. My student and the controller were very helpful and we all conducted great Crew Resource Management during the emergency.

I landed on runway YY for the straight in approach. After landing I taxied off the runway and shut the aircraft down at the nearest ramp off the taxiway.

After securing the aircraft I called the TRACON and told them we landed safely at ZZZ3 airport. The lady on the phone asked me a couple questions to see if anyone was hurt and the rest I cannot remember, due to the rough situation I was in. There was no one hurt! The other instructor who took off behind me on an IFR flight plan was on the same frequency. He then diverted to ZZZ3 airport to be with us.

After the instructor flying the Seminole landed, the A&P mechanic opened up the cowling of the single-engine airplane I was flying and saw that the #4 cylinder cracked. We came into contact with management and they told us to stay at ZZZ3 and relax for a little bit before we return home in the Seminole.

Lessons Learned:

Remember the importance of properly identifying and addressing potential mechanical issues with the aircraft. In this case, the elevated CHT on the number four cylinder was initially dismissed as normal by the instructor, but it was later determined to be a faulty temperature probe.

Even after attempts were made to fix the problem, the issue persisted and eventually led to a hazardous situation.

It is essential to take mechanical issues seriously and conduct thorough inspections to ensure the aircraft is safe to fly before takeoff.

Additionally, it is important to have a plan in place for emergency situations and to communicate effectively with air traffic control to ensure a safe landing.

NOTES:

ENGINE FAILURE ON SHORT FINAL

ASRS, 2014

I departed in a C172 with the intent of completing practice landings at a towered airport at night. The airplane was full of fuel before departing and I added 1 QT of oil, to make the oil level just over 7 QTS total. No noticeable issues on pre-flight and no significant weather. The airplane did not have any noticeable engine issues on the 68 NM trip and seemed to be operating fine.

I contacted Tower roughly 7 miles to the south of the airport at 3,500 MSL, for landing. Tower turned on the runway lights and said, "Report 2 mile final for RWY XX."

I turned on the carburettor heat, reduced the throttle to roughly 1500 RPM, and added 20 degrees of flaps to begin descent for a straight in approach for RWY XX. Still no noticeable issues on descent.

I reported a 2 mile final for RWY XX, and was given clearance to land on RWY XX. To adjust my approach angle, I then added 10 degrees more flaps for a total of 30 degrees of flaps as it appeared I was going in too high.

I continued to descend for the runway and at roughly 200 feet AGL, 70 KIAS, and 0.5 miles from the end of the runway, I slightly reduced the throttle to roughly 1300 RPM to further reduce the approach angle. At this point, the engine stuttered 1-2 times and then completely stopped.

My immediate reaction as the engine stuttered was to push the throttle all the way in to 100% power, but this did not help. With the engine out, the propeller continued to spin, thus indicating a possible starvation condition.

Without engine power, I immediately noticed that I was going to land short of the runway. I quickly removed all flaps and pushed the noise of the aircraft down to increase my airspeed in an attempt to make the runway.

I notified Tower that I had an engine out and was going to attempt to make the runway.

I noticed that I was still going to land short of the runway and was about to hit the MALSR lighting, so I maneuvered the aircraft slightly to the left to avoid impact. I touched down roughly 20 feet from the runway threshold, slightly left of the center line to avoid impact with the approach lighting.

There was no propeller strike and the aircraft rolled up onto RWY XX, where it eventually came to a stop. Tower asked if I needed to declare an emergency and if I was in need of crash assistance. I reported back saying that I was down and safe and did not require assistance. I informed the tower that I would attempt to restart the engine and taxi off of the runway. The engine restarted on the second try, and I taxied off of RWY XX for parking.

On post flight, the aircraft still appeared to be in normal condition with roughly 3/4 of a tank of fuel in each wing. No one was injured and the airplane did not appear to be damaged.

Lessons Learned:

Always be prepared for an emergency. Even though the I did not intend for the engine to fail, I was able to handle the situation because I had prepared for it.

Review and practice emergency procedures regularly. My quick reaction to push the nose down and remove flaps helped to increase airspeed and make the runway.

It is important to remain vigilant and to monitor the aircraft's performance throughout the flight. Remain calm and communicate effectively with air traffic control to help ensure a safe landing.

NOTES:

HOT AND HIGH

CASA, 2015

As a fresh PPL pilot, I was thrilled when I got to navigate across the state all by myself. The sense of achievement I got from sitting in an aluminium tube that hurtles through the sky at 200km/h, and somehow ends up at a predetermined location because of your inputs, was what fascinated me about flying.

It was during February when I started my navigation flights to build hours towards my commercial pilot's licence. Flying from a school based in Melbourne, this meant generally excellent weather and lots of new places to explore.

On a Saturday in February, I had a solo cross-country flight booked in a Cessna 172. The day before the flight, I had put a lot of effort into creating a thorough flight plan to make things easier for me on the flying day. My route would take me up the Kilmore Gap to clear Melbourne control space, then head north west to land at St Arnaud, followed by Echuca for another landing, finally coming back down south to return to my flying school.

Looking at the area forecast on the day, there was nil significant weather until about 4pm, when large cumulonimbus would be building. Not to worry, I should be home by 3pm. Although much to my dislike, the mercury was tipped to reach 43 degrees at 2pm. Wow, what a stinker!

I departed at about 10:30am, and the first segment to St Arnaud was uneventful, albeit a bit hot and bumpy. After completing a few touch and goes, I departed overhead towards my next landing point at Echuca.

It was at this time that I wished I had eaten more before I left, as my stomach was starting to give me grief. The hot and bumpy conditions only made things worse. Then I realised that the aircraft I was flying was fitted with air conditioning; an aftermarket feature designed for a sick pilot like me, flying in 43-degree heat, who was in desperate need of some relief.

I'd never used the air con before, but hey, how hard could it be? 'High' or 'low', 'on' or 'off'? 'I'll take 'high' and 'on' please Mr. Cessna,' I said to myself. Soon I was cool as a cucumber, and happily on my way to Echuca.

It wasn't long before I had forgotten about the aircon, as I focused my attention on preparing for my arrival at Echuca. I joined crosswind for runway 36, and started the before-landing checks. I had always been told to complete these checks without using the paper checklist, as eyes must stay outside in the circuit. As far as I was aware, the 'A' in BOUMFAH only stood for 'autopilot disengaged'. I was soon to be proven very wrong.

As I descended on base, something felt different from normal. I couldn't quite figure out what it was, so I checked all my engine gauges and instruments. Everything looked normal and I continued the approach. As I turned final, there was a large updraft of warm air that caused me to become high and fast on approach. In response to this, I reduced power to idle, extended full flap, and held my aim point.

At 400ft, I glanced down at the tachometer, and was surprised to see a reading of about 350 rpm. The normal reading is about 1500 rpm. A few seconds later, at what I think was about 300ft, the engine and propeller stopped dead. I can't recall exactly what happened after this point, but the next thing I can remember was touching down on the grass area just past the perimeter fence, and rolling onto the sealed runway.

I thought, '*What had just happened? Was that an engine failure? I think it was. What do I do now? Maybe you should try the engine failure checks? Yes, I'll try that.*'

I sat on the runway for about two minutes, trying to restart the engine. But every time I turned the magnetos to start positions, the propeller hardly moved. Then I realised that there was something violently shaking the rudder pedals. 'What could that be? Let's get out and see what the heck is happening.'

As I climbed out, it became obvious that the violent shaking of the rudder pedals was actually my legs shivering as a result of shock. I pushed the aircraft about 200 metres to the nearest taxiway to clear the runway; this was extremely difficult with shaking legs and 43-degree heat. I figured I was in need of food and a drink. I got a taxi into town and purchased lunch.

Upon returning to the airport, I finally built up the courage to get back in the aircraft and try to figure out what was wrong. It wasn't long before I realised that every time I turned on the master switch to try and start the engine, I could hear blaring fans from behind the glare shield, and feel air being blown onto my face. This explained the unusual feeling I had on base, and why I couldn't start the engine on the ground. The aircon was still switched on.

As it turns out, the 'A' in the before landing checklist was also marked as 'Air conditioning—off/not applicable', although this was not listed as a read back item, so I had never actually used it before. After finally starting up, I completed three sets of run-ups, not finding any problems with the engine, taxied to the runway for my delayed return home.

On the way home, I entered the flight plan into the GPS and turned on autopilot. I had had enough navigating for that day. Unfortunately, like a final curse from the gods of aviation, I encountered severe turbulence from building cumulonimbus on the way home. My late departure from Echuca had caused me to encounter the forecast storms developing on the way home. The result of this was my lunch making an unscheduled exit through my mouth just before landing back at home. Finally, I touched down. I have never been happier to be home.

Lessons Learned:

On the following Monday, I submitted an incident report and discussed the events with the chief instructor. He believed the engine stoppage could have been caused by the air conditioning taking power away from the engine. As I had reduced power to idle on short final, the rpm had dropped to such a slow speed that the engine simply stopped.

I believe that due to the conditions on the day, a very high-density altitude meant the engine's power output was already significantly reduced. This combined with low idle speed and the aircon belt taking power away from the crankshaft, was enough to cause engine failure.

It haunts me to think what the outcome might have been had I been on a runway with trees on the approach, or lost power just a few seconds earlier than had happened. Nowadays, I always check for Air Conditioning OFF before any landing, and more importantly, I give the checklists a lot more respect. I love flying, and I hope to make it a safe career for myself. Hopefully my story will cause others to learn from my mistake, and maybe even save a life.

NOTES:

SMOKE AND SPARKS IN THE CABIN

ASRS, 2018

I was flying from ZZZ to ZZZ1 for pattern work, and on final for the first touch and go the PFD indicated it was running on battery and the Alternator Field circuit breaker was popped. I reset the circuit breaker, broke out of the pattern and started heading back to ZZZ as a precaution. The Alternator Field circuit breaker would not stay engaged more than 1-2 minutes, where I would reset it again.

I was talking to ATC Approach the whole time for flight following and gave them a heads up on the situation of a possible impending electrical failure, and they in turn gave ZZZ Tower a heads up on the situation.

Getting closer to ZZZ I turned off all unnecessary lights and the Number 2 radio just to conserve power. Once I contacted ZZZ Tower they cleared me for a right downwind for XX. Right as I was coming up on the north/east shore of the reservoir there was a "pop" and a large puff of acrid electrical smelling smoke with sparks emanating from behind/below the panel on my side of the aircraft.

I immediately advised ATC about the smoke in the cockpit and told them I needed the runway right now and I was headed for Runway YY. They cleared traffic away and me to land, and which point I radioed that I was turning off the electrical/master.

I was alternating looking down at the panel/my feet for any more sparks/smoke and ahead of me to setup for landing. I opened the window for some fresh air and was able to land safely.

Then with the aircraft on the ground and under control I pulled the mixture and fuel control valve off. I coasted off to the ramp and evacuated the aircraft and the fire equipment soon came. The fire department confirmed there was no active fire with a thermal camera and left quickly for another call.

Lessons Learned:

I believe constantly resetting the popped circuit breaker might have been a contributing factor to the smoke/sparks. We have been having trouble with the Alternator Field circuit breaker for a while and mechanics would check it out but the root cause was not found so the issue would recur.

Because of this and the seemingly innocuous nature of the continued situation it had become a standard process almost to reset it every time it pops, which is something that I will not do in the future more than once.

NOTES:

ENGINE FAILURE AFTER TAKEOFF

ASRS, 2017

I was on a training flight with a Student Pilot getting check ride ready, which was to take part two days later. Before takeoff I did my usual check with the student, oil was at 6 qts and fuel was topped off (53 Gal) as a safety precaution.

The flight was a typical training flight, took off from [home airport], did some ground reference maneuvers in the area, followed by landings in ZZZ airport, an uncontrolled field. After two landings in the pattern, I told the student to prepare for a short field takeoff and since he was getting ready for check ride everything was by the book, from checklists to airspeed and Oil temperature and pressure call outs.

On this one, I said, "ENGINE FAILED", student took appropriate action and stopped the aircraft, pulled throttle and said in real life he would pull the mixture and the appropriate checklist. I was satisfied and we further discussed eventualities if the engine did fail on takeoff roll, below 1000 feet and after that.

After this simulated abort takeoff, we decided to return to home airport. On this final departure, again everything by the book, proper non-towered radio calls, checklists and use of runway space. On takeoff roll, on the Vx climb, I was satisfied and continued with a clear of obstacle call, the student then pitched for Vy.

About 3 seconds after, I heard a BANG! I immediately looked at the tires to see if they popped, the oil pressure and temperature, they were green. Simultaneously the aircraft began to shake and vibrate violently. I looked at the VSI and saw the climb go from +800 FPM down to barely +50 FPM.

My student looked at me and said, "I've lost the engine...", I took over controls and added full power, Idle, then power again. Nothing changed and clearly there was a problem.

At this point, I'm still maintaining heading, airspeed began to decrease and I said, "Confirm engine loss....", student said, "confirm!". I had no choice, I had to put it down.

I told the student, "Seatbelt on tight, door open now, I have this". Immediately, I knew from experience that I could not land this plane straight given the speed and rate of drop and ground roll. I banked about 15-20 Degrees left and slipped the plane down to the corner of a field and put the plane diagonally off the runway numbers, an approximate 305 heading.

On touchdown, I had flaps full and hit the ground right as the stall horn went off, touchdown was rough but I held the back pressure in and did a basic soft field landing. Since I had never done a real grass landing before I did not apply brakes and knew the plane will stop eventually.

When the plane came to a full stop, I told the student, "After landing checklist now!" He ran it pulled full emergency cutoff, fuel selected off and ran the checklist. I had my left hand on the fire extinguisher and my right hand had the checklist in hand ready for a fire, explosion, oil spewing, whatever come may.

To our luck, nothing came after, so when we got out, I said, "Fuel check". We had 42 Gal total and Oil was still around 6 quarts.

Lessons Learned:

Post incident:

On my inspection, no oil leaked, no sign of outside damage. I called the owner/flight school and did a post check of the exterior, no damage to the propeller, wheel pants, tires, or fuselage. Luckily we found a crack in cylinder #4 next to the spark plug which caused the Partial Power Loss and vibration issue with the aircraft. 65 feet remained between the aircraft and a fence, luckily an airport tenant saw and heard the incident so he immediately sprang in to help and get a tow to get our plane out.

Since my student and I were in the check ride prep mode, I believe that this led to the great outcome of our flight. The issue could not be prevented since it was a maintenance problem, so my job as an instructor was done and had I made any calls differently, surely the result would have been bad. My student remained calm and collected and I think I acted appropriately given the situation I had.

I know this is not standard, but I do train my SEL students for private at a higher standard and although not a required procedure except for MEL, I train my students to react if an engine loss occurs 800 feet to return to the field in the opposite direction. My student said that me practicing this with him helped in alleviating the fear if the plane lost power and said attributed to the issue.

<u>NOTES:</u>

ENGINE PROBLEM DIVERSION

ASRS, 2018

I was pilot at the controls, while my copilot was the pilot in command for this leg. He is an instrument rated pilot, with 1200+ hours, and we had been flying the second leg of our journey.

We departed and began our climb to 7,000 feet. At about 6,000 feet we ran into engine roughness and shaking, fairly substantial. We levelled off and began to troubleshoot the issue after notifying ATC.

After full rich and adjusting throttles and re-leaning we regained smooth run and continued climb. We reached 7,000 feet and were able to continue on course. Oil pressures and fuel flow were fine. We monitored those closely.

Ten miles north of ZZZ the engine issues returned. We began to troubleshoot roughness by swapping tanks, re-leaning, but could find no direct relationship between symptoms and inputs on the system (changing inputs did not affect performance). We asked for assistance and vectors and went to ZZZ. Doing the turn-descent we lost all power briefly, and regained it. By now we advised ATC.

The engine resumed running with inconsistent roughness and performed reasonably smooth in the final stages of arrival. We were able to land with power.

During the descent we lost communications on Radio 1 somewhere between 4,000 and 3,000 feet. We were unable to hear ATC and assumed they could not hear us. We had already configured Tower at ZZZ into Radio 2, and we swapped to that, reestablishing communications. I confirmed they were aware we had advised ATC and were inbound for Runway XX, the most direct runway in sight.

Engine performance was mixed, producing what appeared like full power, but neither of us was certain whether that was actually the case. The winds were 20+ knots and we were landing with a major crosswind, unreliable engine, wind shear and gusts. Not the best landing, but one that worked and got us on the ground safely.

Upon landing, we were able to taxi to FBO under our own power and eventually have a mechanic do an initial assessment.

At the time of the initial diagnosis the mechanic confirmed poor compression in Cylinder 1, and experienced violent shaking at full power that was yet to be isolated or understood. The plane was left at ZZZ for diagnosis and repairs.

Lessons Learned:

Always be vigilant during flight, even when everything seems to be going well. The pilot in command noticed the engine roughness and shaking at 6,000 feet and immediately began troubleshooting the issue.

Communication is crucial during emergencies. The loss of communication on Radio 1 added a layer of complexity to an already stressful situation. It is important to have a backup plan in place for communication in case of equipment failure.

It is important to be prepared for unexpected situations.

NOTES:

MY ENGINE STARTED RUNNING ROUGH

ASRS, 2018

The aircraft had three occupants; a private pilot in the left seat, a private pilot passenger in the rear seat and myself in the right seat acting as a supervising instructor. The intent of the flight was for the pilot in the left seat to refresh currency and proficiency prior to a cross-country flight planned for later in the day. The pilot in the left seat had completed one circuit in the traffic pattern and had departed upwind following a touch and go on Runway XX.

On initial climbout, I noted that the engine was not making full power, indicating only 2030 RPM. After checking with the pilot and verifying correctness of throttle position, I took control of the airplane with annunciation inside the cockpit, and promptly [advised ATC]. The aircraft was approximately 50 feet AGL at this point.

The engine was running rough. I determined that we had a slight positive climb rate. I elected to climb while looking for possible landing sites straight ahead. After the aircraft was above the power lines to the right (~400 feet AGL), I turned the airplane slightly to the right and started a left teardrop back to the airport.

I was simultaneously assessing whether there was anything to our left that was workable as a landing spot. I was also aware that the Tower had cleared us to land on any runway, and was clearing airspace for us, directing traffic in the pattern away from and above our flight path. Once I knew we could glide to Runway XY, I closed the throttle, deployed full flaps and started side-slipping and S-turning to lose altitude to make the runway.

My attempts to lose altitude were insufficient to make a landing with adequate runway. At the time it was unclear to me why this was so, in spite of the relatively light tailwind (~5 kts) we were dealing with. After seeing that I had only one third of the Runway XY remaining and we were still about 10 to 15 feet off the ground, I made the very uncomfortable decision to apply all available power from the engine and attempt to 'go-around.'

Due to the flaps still being fully deployed, and the airplane only running up to ~2000 RPM, the aircraft didn't accelerate or climb well, barely clearing the fence south of the airport boundary.

In a moment of haste, I retracted all the flaps, and heard the stall warning horn chirp momentarily - a glance at airspeed indicator showed ~55 knots. Because the flaps are electric, I brought the flap switch down to a partial setting, which likely just paused the retraction I had commanded seconds earlier. I then retracted them fully after a few more seconds.

I deviated slightly to the right on the shallow climb-out hoping to put the airplane down near the bike tracks south of the airport. Because of rising terrain in this area, our AGL altitude was perceived to be no higher than 50 feet. I was weighing my decision-making between landing off airport straight ahead or returning to the airport because I was unsure how long the engine would continue running.

The pilot-passenger in the back seat suggested heading to [an alternate airport] but it was unclear if we could climb past the power lines, so I discounted this.

I started a left teardrop turn again to the airport for Runway XX, maneuvering at the level of power lines that run along the east of the airport.

Once we were oriented towards Runway XX, I let the airplane continue climbing until just above the normal glide path indicator. I closed the throttle and applied flaps over the pond just short of Runway XX. To the best of my recollection, airspeed was about 75 knots at this point. Best glide was expected to be just under 70, and I was intentionally keeping some margin above this airspeed.

What all occupants remember is that during this power reduction, the engine was not idling. It was running at 1600 RPM and had smoothened out noticeably than when it was making partial power at the full throttle setting.

Suspecting that the airplane's engine was not going to idle as expected and also noting that our glide path was causing us to approach the runway faster than desired at 70 to 75 kts, I anticipated needing to kill the engine upon touchdown.

We touched down about on the runway in the vicinity [of] taxiway X. I had the left seat occupant turn off the ignition switch as soon as the wheels touched down. I applied maximum braking to stop the airplane about 50 feet short of the airport boundary fence, in the overrun area of the runway.

No injuries or damage to the aircraft resulted. An airport service vehicle helped tow the airplane off the runway. At the time of writing, maintenance personnel had done diagnostic run-ups after our landing on the engine and indicated one of the magnetos may have been malfunctioning.

Lessons Learned:

Factors affecting my decision making (beyond the inherently unexpected nature of the emergency):

1. Rehearsing for engine failure after takeoff (EFATO) has always been 'full power loss' in my training, and my instructors have maintained that the best course of action is to try to land straight ahead if below pattern altitude. I had some rehearsal for EFATO was as recently as 2 months prior to this event, during checkout of another aircraft type with an instructor.

2. I was acutely aware during the emergency that the 'impossible turn' attempted by pilots after EFATO-type events usually don't work because of the altitude loss during the 180. In spite of all these points, I set myself up for it anyway, because the engine was making some power, and I was able to keep us high enough for an approach to the 'downwind' runway.

3. I deliberately stopped at step 1 of the typical emergency checklist, "Fly the airplane." I reached an initial conclusion in flight that this was likely an induction or ignition issue, with mechanical failure being less likely because of the following: I had good fuel flow, good oil pressure, and engine vibration was not jarring. Because I didn't have the luxury of altitude, I did not touch the ignition switch in case I killed the engine without a landing spot to aim for.

4. Other than the airport, it was very clear that there were no good options to ditch in the vicinity. Power lines running north to south, along the east of the airport 'boxed us in' over marshes to avoid populated areas.

5. During the second attempt at landing, I wondered if the throttle linkage was preventing me from truly idling the engine, and if this made a tailwind approach on Runway XY impossible. Suspecting this, I anticipated needing to kill the ignition even on Runway XX, where we landed much farther down the runway than is standard.

6. It is entirely possible that the engine was running at 1600 RPM purely from the higher-than best glide airspeed I was maintaining. However, this was hard to accept in the moment since the engine had also 'smoothed out' when the throttle handle was pulled to the closed position. The others on board shared my surprise when I pointed this out on short final. The effect of tailwind on the glidepath was difficult to account for when most landings are attempted into the wind under normal circumstances.

7. My assessment is that my relatively low time in C172s was a contributing factor in inaccurately anticipating how well the aircraft can glide, slip, and slow down with flaps. This was especially true for the attempt on Runway XX. If I were to guess, I'd say that I was faster than recommended for both the approaches I attempted after [advising ATC], likely overcompensating against the spectre of full engine failure, which could have been expected at any time.

8. [The airport]'s runway is short; at only 2,400 feet, it is possible that I could have made it down on something about twice as long during the tailwind landing attempt on Runway XY. It is also possible that, had this issue occurred on a longer runway, a landing straight ahead would have put us back on the runway.

9. Because of task saturation associated with flying the airplane, it was very difficult to respond to all information from ATC. However, I was listening during the whole incident and aware that ATC was offering relevant information, helpful clearances, and clearing the airspace for us.

10. I surprised myself with the near-subconscious decision to announce control of the aircraft and [advising ATC] within seconds of realizing the engine was not behaving.

11. Declaring was a call for help - one that Tower effectively and professionally responded to. I hope that others finding themselves in such a situation are trained to do so without hesitation.

<u>NOTES:</u>

LOSS OF ENGINE POWER

ASRS, 2018

I was flying heading 355 northbound towards the bay at 1100 feet, picking up the ATIS that was at that time information GOLF (G).

Shortly after correcting the altimeter setting [while] listening [to] the ATIS, [I was] cruising at 2350 RPM with the mixture full rich position, the engine quit with a COMPLETE loss of power and the propeller at 1800 RPM with a complete engine silence. The nose of the aircraft was pitching down between five and ten degrees and my immediate action was [to] turn off in the audio panel COMM 2 (ATIS). COMM 1 was already [on] ZZZ Tower.

During the engine silence, I said, "TOWER, Aircraft X MAYDAY MAYDAY MAYDAY" with my left hand on the [push to talk] and the right hand changing the fuel tank selector to right from both and mixture back 40 percent throttle full open.

The event took place in the southern side of a hospital at 9 o'clock, the highway had plenty of cars both ways, and at 3 o'clock there was a hotel.

After the mayday call, ZZZ Tower called me back, and I had a lazy engine response at 950 feet altimeter indication and 90 of indicated airspeed.

With the mixture back 40 percent, my full power setting was 2300 RPM when normally [it] is 2500. [The] aircraft was climbing slowly to 1500 feet to be in a safer altitude in case of another similar event.

I was cleared to land Runway XX straight in and the engine tried to quit two times during the approach in long final and in short final.

Lessons Learned:

Next day I spoke to the technician and he told me in the phone call that he changed spark plugs and there was a carb heat wire malfunction and I understood that an intake tube was melted and it was changed.

<u>NOTES:</u>

LOSS OF POWER AFTER TAKEOFF

ASRS, 2018

Upon initially approaching the plane I noticed a small drip coming from the right wing's fuel sump. I called maintenance over to come look at it. After they jerked it open and closed a few times the drip stopped. Maintenance said there is no issue with taking it up flying.

I continued with my preflight. I taxied to the run up area just before Runway XX and proceeded to do my run up. During the run up there were no indications of anything wrong. So I entered the runway and began my takeoff. During my roll all engine instruments were in the green and everything was going great.

At 500 ft AGL my engine started to sputter. I immediately put the carb heat on and verified my mixture and power were at full. No effect. I immediately [advised on] CTAF and told everyone my intentions and emergency and begun a circle to land for Runway YY.

I touched down on Runway YY with no issues but then my engine cut out immediately after touch down. It took a few tries to restart my engine but I finally did but found I needed half power in just to keep the engine running.

I taxied back to the FBO and parked the aircraft. Immediately upon exiting the aircraft I smelled fuel and noticed fuel pouring out from under the front cowling in the vicinity of the nose gear.

I wrote the plane up for maintenance and told them of my problem.

Lessons Learned:

As I am writing this report I am unsure of what was wrong. Best guess is the fuel line. I had a funny feeling that something might happen during my flight when I had maintenance come out to check the fuel sump drain. One thing that saved this from becoming an accident with an actual engine failure in flight was my swift decision making to immediately turn to the other runway and not take any chances. If I hesitated maybe another 30 seconds to come to a decision my engine would have surely quit in midair.

<u>NOTES:</u>

CHAPTER 10

AIRWORTHINESS & MAINTENANCE

"Hard to stay awake in dark place – can't use radio – can't use electric fuel pump. Pump all gasoline by hand, using minimum lights... Don't realize how necessary this power until all of a sudden – sitting in the dark – no lights in panel to fly by – flashlight burning out – can't see to fix the trouble if you could fix at all."

John Cook

Flight Endurance World Record holder with Robert Timm

(64 days, 22 hours, & 19 minutes in a Cessna 172)

1958, Las Vegas

SEAT FAILURE ON TAKE-OFF

CHIRP, 2016

On Sunday 16 October 2016, a Cessna 150 crashed at Bourn airfield on take-off and I sent a text to my flying partner saying that I thought it could be the classic case of seat lock failure. This is where the seat lock is not fully engaged and as the pilot rotates it can rush back. The pilot hangs onto the yoke and the aircraft pitches up, stalls and spins in.

The following weekend we both arrived at the airfield and again discussed the possible reason for the crash. We checked out my Cessna and prepared for start-up. As I am aware of the seat failure situation, I always lock the pin in place and then "rattle" the seat back and forth to check that it is locked.

We taxied out to the warm up area and I carried out my pre-flight checks. Again as part of my checks I "rattled" the seat. I then lined up on the runway, did a few more checks and opened the throttle. As I approached takeoff speed I rotated the aircraft and when we were about 10 feet off the ground, my seat suddenly shot backwards.

My arms were at full stretch and I could not reach the rudder pedals or the throttle (I am short).

My co-pilot shouted at me, "Nose Down!" and I shouted back, "Take Control!"

He pushed the yoke forward and the aircraft wallowed then went downwards picking up speed. We cleared the runway and climbed out and he asked what had happened.

We did a circuit and I asked him if he was OK landing from the right seat and he said, "Possibly." Not a good answer, so I pulled my seat forward and locked the pin again. I noticed that it did not have any tension from the spring that pulls it downwards and keeps it in place. We decided that I would land the aircraft but he would follow me through and take control for a go around if necessary. I landed OK and taxied back to the ramp.

Upon examination, we found that the spring had broken and was hanging on one point. I took out the spring and thought I would check how bad the spring was. I got a pair of pliers to bend the top of the spring which snapped off. I bent another bit and that snapped off. The spring which I assume was the same age as the aircraft as it was painted the same colour as the seat (51 years), was completely metal fatigued.

Lessons Learned:

I have now changed both front seat springs but it has occurred to me that the springs have a limited life and they should perhaps be replaced over a certain period, say 10 years. Unfortunately, Cessna charge £25 for each spring which may discourage owners to replace them at regular intervals.

A further point is that we as pilots who often fly as P2 should practise flying from the right seat in case of emergency, especially landing and in a crosswind. The situation is so different from what one is used to.

Even though the accident the week previously was fresh in my mind, my seat rushing back still came as a shock and if my co-pilot had not taken control immediately, the situation could have been worse.

CHIRP Comment:

Loss of control incidents are reportable as Mandatory Occurrence Reports (MORs) and this reporter had complied with the requirement. Since seat slippage can occur on any aircraft with a moveable seat, it is vital to check the security of the seat, as this pilot did, whether or not the seat has recently been moved. Although the incident was caused by a failure of the lock pin spring, there is a history of problems with other aspects of the seat and a relevant and extant FAA Airworthiness Directive FAA AD 2011-10-09 that applies to many models of Cessna aircraft. The summary extract says:

> "SUMMARY: We are superseding an existing airworthiness directive (AD) for Cessna Aircraft Company (Cessna) 150, 152, 170, 172, 175, 177, 180, 182, 185, 188, 190, 195, 206, 207, 210, T303, 336, and 337 series airplanes. That AD currently requires repetitive inspections and replacement of parts, if necessary, of the seat rail and seat rail holes; seat pin engagement; seat rollers, washers, and axle bolts or bushings; wall thickness of roller housing and the tang; and lock pin springs. This new AD requires retaining all of the actions from the previous AD and adding steps to the inspection procedures in the previous AD. This AD was prompted by added steps to the inspection procedures, added revised figures, and clarification of some of the existing steps. We are issuing this AD to prevent seat slippage or the seat roller housing from departing the seat rail, which may consequently cause the pilot/co-pilot to be unable to reach all the controls. This failure could lead to the pilot/co-pilot losing control of the airplane."

It should be noted that the FAA AD 2011-10-09 inspections and any actions arising (cleaning, replacement due to wear, cracking etc.) should continue to be performed every 12 months or every 100 HR TIS, whichever comes sooner, and the work should be carried out by a qualified aircraft engineer.

<u>NOTES:</u>

FIXATED RESOLVING THE PROBLEM NOT AVIATING

ASRS, 2019

On an IFR flight from to ZZZ, I encountered a glideslope indicator failure when established on the ILS 21L into ZZZ. Worse-than-forecasted and deteriorating weather conditions plus climbs for traffic avoidance with ZZZ Center had consumed more fuel than planned and had burned all of fuel carried in excess of fuel to alternate [plus] 45 minutes.

Once glideslope failure was determined, I was vectored for one more attempt of the ILS after troubleshooting the VLOC/GPS [VOR/Localizer/Global Positioning System] selector for user error.

After determining that pilot error wasn't the cause of the failure, I told ZZZ Approach at that point, I was going to my filed alternate of ZZZ1. Once on track to ZZZ1, I determined that winds aloft created roughly 25 kts stronger headwind than forecasted and with our fuel situation would prevent us from getting to ZZZ1.

At that point with roughly 8 gallons of fuel indicated total, I [advised ATC] for low fuel.

ZZZ Approach assisted me with determining whether at surrounding airports and found that ZZZ2 had ceilings about 100 feet above minimums for the RNAV 29. ZZZ1 also has ASR [Airport Surveillance Radar] for the RNAV 29. I elected for the ASR on the RNAV 29.

ZZZ1 Approach controllers executed the ASR approach from the FAF of ZZZZZ. I gained visual of the field environment at the minimums of 1,540 feet and quickly gained visual of the runway at about 1/4 nm from the approach end of Runway 29 and about 1/8 nm right of centerline. A landing from minimums was conducted using normal maneuvers to Runway 29.

Lessons Learned:

This event was a great example of the Swiss Cheese model of risk management; enough small issues accumulated that a larger issue occurred. During preflight planning, I had selected a cruising altitude of 4,000 feet due to the favorable winds and had noted that higher altitudes had much worse headwinds.

When ZZZ Center issued us a climb to 8,000 feet, I had just checked fuel and we were burning less fuel than planned and was indicating more fuel on board than planned at the last waypoint. I believe this set a confirmation bias that led me to believe the fuel savings up to that point would cancel out with the climb and added headwind, and for the most part it did.

Once we started our descent down to 6,000 feet, we were still on track with indicated vs. planned fuel on board, but headwinds didn't lighten up at lower altitudes as forecasted. This is when our indicated fuel on board dropped below planned fuel on board.

At this point, I didn't see this as an issue because I had planned on having over an hour of fuel more. However, the failure of the glideslope indicator and increased headwind on track to the alternate were the last links in the chain of issues that arose the closer we get to ZZZ.

Knowing that fuel had already dropped below what was planned, I should have made the decision as soon as the glideslope indicator failed to go to the filed alternate, but I got too fixated resolving the problem and was convinced that I improperly set up the instruments that I accepted a vector for another attempt instead of taking control of the situation and immediately diverting to the alternate. Having done that, I could have avoided another 20-30 minutes of vectoring and would have had the fuel to get to ZZZ1.

NOTES:

ALTERNATOR AND LOST COMMS FAILURE

ASRS, 2016

I performed a preflight inspection, and found nothing unusual. Upon attempting to start the engine, the battery did not seem to have enough cranking power. I assumed this was due to the cold weather, and requested a GPU Jump Start from the FBO. On the second attempt, the engine started, and the GPU was disconnected.

I continued my after starting-engine check-list (and put my cellular phone in Airplane Mode), and all seemed normal. I made it a special point to check the ammeter, and it appeared to be charging slightly. I also have a "cigar lighter" USB charger/voltmeter that I use as a secondary reference to the battery health, and I remember it being around 13 volts (which seemed normal from past experiences).

I received my IFR clearance, performed my run-up, and proceeded for normal flight. I departed from ZZZ.

Departure began normally, I was handed off from ZZZ Tower to ZZZ Departure while climbing to 8000. I was then handed off to [new departure frequency] had been told to climb maintain 9000.

ZZZ Departure instructed me to climb maintain 13,000 feet. I initiated my climb and keyed my mic to read-back my instruction. As I keyed the mic, my #1 radio (a Garmin 430W) went out. I switched my panel to my #2 radio and tuned it, I heard ZZZ Approach repeating my climb instruction. I again keyed my mic to confirm with a read-back, and the #2 radio (Garmin SL-30) went out. I reached for my handheld and attempted to make call out to ZZZ Departure, but my attempted failed. I powered off the hand-held to conserve battery when I realized that I was unable to transmit for anyone to reach me. I cycled the power on each radio, as well as the radio master in attempts to re-establish communications. None of my efforts worked. The Transponder (Garmin GTX-345) failed to come back up after one of the power cycles. I then left the power off to the avionics for a couple minutes and turned off all but the transponder with hopes that when turning back on the transponder would have enough power to send a signal. After various attempts, the transponder did come up, and I squawked 7600, and the transponder cut back out.

I reverted to training (that I remembered), and that was to fly my assigned clearance. Being my last instruction was to climb and maintain 13,000, and that was my filed altitude. I levelled off at 13,000. I turned on my Oxygen tank about 15 minutes after crossing 12,500 feet - and maintained oxygen flow for the remainder of the flight. I proceeded navigating with my iPad and its built-in GPS. At ZZZ VOR, I turned Direct to ZZZ1.

As has been instilled in me, *Aviate, Navigate and Communicate* - I established that the aircraft was safe to continue flight, with the noted electrical issue so I flew it. I navigated with the iPad, and established course heading to maintain for the remainder of the flight to ZZZ1. I then decided to attempt to communicate with my cellular phone, so I turned off the "airplane mode."

Note, I included my cell phone number in comments of the flight plan when it was filed.

Later I noticed that I received a voice mail message from ZZZ TRACON stated that they saw I was on my flight plan route at 13,000, and that I was out of their airspace, their concern was the busier airspace near ZZZ1, they asked for a call-back. I was able to have strong enough signal at the time I read the message to make an outgoing call. I called ZZZ Center at the number provided. Informed them that I was following my clearance and intended to continue to ZZZ1 at 13,000. I provided a position report and advised of the electrical issue. I also reported that the conditions were VMC. I was told to call ZZZ TRACON upon landing. Additionally, I requested the phone number for ZZZ1 ATC (and was provided Tower phone number).

I received a voice message from ZZZ1 Center advising that I would be entering a MOA and to call them. As soon as I was able to get a call out, I did call them. I gave them a position report and confirmed that I would maintain 13,000 within 100 feet.

ZZZ1 Center called and left me a few messages that they lost radar and when they picked it up again and an additional position report request. The last of their messages requested that I maintain 13000. They provided the call-back number. I made several attempts to communicate with them, however the cellular signal did not allow the call to go through. There was one point where I had brief communications and was able to get a position report to them.

I continued my flight directly to ZZZ1. Within 10 miles of ZZZ1, I was unable to get cellular signal to call Tower. I used my handheld to get the ATIS information L, and then switched to Tower frequency.

When within about 4 miles (at 13,000 feet) I was able to contact Tower using the Handheld, but it was broken. I copied that I was cleared to land Runway 1. I needed to lose 12,500 feet of altitude. I crossed midfield and started my descent over a right-pattern for runway 1, applied a forward slip to lose more altitude quicker. Continued a right-pattern, and crossed the runway threshold around 6000.

I made one more right pattern to lose the remaining altitude, and during that time, I heard tower advise me that I was cleared to land any runway. I made a normal landing on Runway 1, taxied off where emergency vehicles were awaiting me.

I taxied to the FBO, parked, and shut down the aircraft. I then noticed I had an additional call from ZZZ1 Approach asking me to call. Once the aircraft was secured I called ZZZ1 Approach, and we discussed what happened. Then I called ZZZ TRACON (per request from initial communication with ZZZ Center via phone), and they asked me why I didn't squawk 7600 immediately. I explained that I attempted to cycle the radios first.

Lessons Learned:

I asked the FBO's mechanic to check the electrical system before I used the aircraft again. I was informed that the alternator was generating 12.6 Volts, while it should be above 13. He recharged the battery, but his belief is that over time it has been slowly discharging because the alternator was not producing enough to support all the avionics. The alternator was last replaced with a new one in 2015.

After landing, I was reminded that the IFR Lost Communications procedure in VMC is to land at the earliest practicable airport. I believe that turning back to the ZZZ area would have been more dangerous without communications. I could have landed at ZZZ2, or many other airports along the route, but I kept them in mind if I needed to deviate for a more serious emergency.

With my mind stuck in the mantra of *Aviate, Navigate, and Communicate* - I was focused on safely flying the aircraft, assuring that my navigation (with the iPad) was accurate, and attempting to communicate with ATC facilities via phone.

I did the best that I could with the resources available to me, but I do understand that it caused undue burden on ATC facilities.

NOTES:

GEAR UP LANDING

ASRS, 2018

This was a night flight with the purpose of renewing my night currency for carrying passengers.

The week before I completed a BFR in a C172RG and I decided to immediately get night current. On this flight I was a little fatigued but pushed on...

My preflight included mounting my iPad to the yoke which provided Foreflight navigation information. The iPad also blocked some of the instruments including the gear position lights.

On downwind I delayed lowering the landing gear to extend downwind for approach. I forgot to go back and lower the gear and was reminded when the aircraft landed gear up.

I was the only person onboard and was not injured. The aircraft sustained propeller damage and scrapes on the bottom.

Lessons Learned:

I believe that positioning the iPad in a way so as not to obstruct the gear position lights would have prevented this incident.

It would have been beneficial to fly with an instructor on my first night flight in over a year in an aircraft that I had on 1.3 recent hours in.

I hope that this input serves to prevent a repeat.

NOTES:

FAILURE OF THE LANDING GEAR TO EXTEND

ASRS, 2018

At around mid-morning my student and I started up the aircraft and taxied out of the ramp. We then proceeded to do normal operations and test. After all the test were complete, and the engine had warmed, we then took off to the south. We then proceeded south over 10 miles and did a series of maneuvers in preparation [for] my students CFI check ride.

After we finished up on maneuvers, we then came back into the airport for landing practice. After completion of the first touch and go, we continued in the pattern for another landing.

Upon reaching mid-field downwind, as my student placed the gear selector down, we realized we didn't have a down and locked gear indication (one green light). My student then asked the tower for an east heading to work on our issue.

After running the checklist, "Landing gear fails to extend checklist", this did not fix our issue. We have now realized by looking out the window that the right main is swinging freely in a mid-travel position.

At this time, we realized we needed more time and space to analyze our issue. At this point, I have taken over the radio and my student is flying. We then asked the tower for a turn to the south to clear his airspace and further work on the issue.

As my student was flying to the south, I gave tower my phone number and asked him to get one of FBO mechanics to call me. After talking to the mechanic, we confirmed that we could try and slip the plane to get the gear to lock down but the chances were it was not going to swing into position. We then talked about a "gear up landing" and how that would be a less risky landing than landing with 2 of 3 gear down.

Once I was off the phone with the mechanic, I told my student to climb to 5000 feet to get some altitude under us before we tried a series of slips and pitch changes to try and swing the gear into place. All of these techniques did not work.

We then asked Tower for a low approach over the field and headed back to the airport. We asked for the low approach to see if the mechanic could see anything different from his viewpoint. We wanted to see if he saw anything out of the ordinary besides the gear not fully down and locked (something else blocking the gear from extending fully). After passing him, he said the nose wheel and left main appear down but the right main was not fully extended and locked.

We now had all the confirmation we needed that we were going to have to do a gear up landing. We then declared PIC authority under FAR 91.3 and proceeded to the south once more to wait for emergency crews to arrive.

Once established on a South heading, I took control of the aircraft and asked my student to pull out the POH (Pilot's Operating Handbook) and double check the emergency procedures and see if there was anything that differed between our checklist and the POH. After confirming the checklists were identical and there were no other procedures we then discussed how putting the gear up was the safest way to land the aircraft in the situation we were given.

Once the emergency services arrived, we headed back to do a gear up landing.

On the downwind leg, we cycled the gear up. The gear all came up but the right main. It dangled in a half travel position. We confirmed this with tower and then told them we would no longer talk to them once we turned final. This being because we were going to turn off the master and all electrical components prior to landing.

After turning final we turned all electrical systems off. Once the field was made, we then pulled the mixture to idle/cutoff and cracked the exit doors. I then glided the plane to the runway and held it right above the runway until it got slow enough it couldn't fly anymore. We then impacted the runway with the planes belly.

The plane skidded to a stop and my student and I exited towards the tail as previously briefed.

Lessons Learned:

Always be prepared for emergencies: It is important to have emergency procedures and checklists (POH) readily available and to know them well. We were able to quickly reference the appropriate checklist and procedures to assess the situation and make a decision.

Maintain clear communication: We were in constant communication with the tower and mechanics, keeping them updated on the situation and seeking their advice. We communicated clearly with the tower that we would no longer be able to talk due to turning off the electrical systems.

Stay calm and focused: Work together to assess the situation and make a safe landing.

Prioritize safety: In an emergency situation, safety should always be the top priority. A gear up landing was the safest option given the circumstances.

NOTES:

ASYMMETRIC FLAP RESULTED IN A DIFFICULT LANDING

ASRS, 2018

My student and I were practicing maneuvers. When we were about to turn left we looked out the window and saw that the left flap was down to at least 20 degrees and had serious structural damage.

I checked to see if both flaps were at the same setting but the right flap was up. The flap lever was in the o degree position. I don't know what had caused it. I suspected that something had hit it because it looked severely damaged. Potentially a bird because I don't know what else it could have been. I've never been in this situation before.

I cut the lesson short and headed back to the airport for a full stop right away. To maintain control I had to press the right rudder pedal more and put in right aileron to counter the plane's movement. If I were to let the controls go it felt as if the plane would have rolled to the right and yawed to the left.

I informed Tower Controller that we were inbound for a landing and that we had a left flap that was down and thus asymmetrical flaps. I wanted to give a sense of urgency.

We were given the closest runway to us and I was okay with that as I just wanted to get down safely and as soon as possible.

As we descended I did what I needed to keep the airplane at approximately 70 knots and aligned with the runway centerline.

When we touched down the plane rolled to the left uncontrollably and made attempting a go around impossible without complete loss of control.

I applied braking action to slow the plane down and keep us on the centerline and all my efforts were spent on slowing the plane down safely on the runway. The plane was uncontrollably being pulled left towards the grass and I did everything I could to stop it from getting off and as safely as I could. At the edge of the runway I was pressing on the brakes and still the plane would not stop heading towards the left. I was finally able to get the plane to a full stop. Tower then gave us instructions that we were to taxi onto a taxiway and contact Ground Control. I told the Tower Controller that we were in the grass and that we might have struck a light. We contacted Ground Control and were given instructions to taxi to our ramp.

Lessons Learned:

Next time, I would remain calm, declare an emergency, ask for the longer runway and land on the side of center-line where there the flap isn't lowered to adjust for the additional asymmetrical drag and how it affects the airplane upon landing. I would also encourage more literature on how to deal with asymmetrical flap failures as well as an emergency checklist item for such a situation in pilot operating handbooks or in the FAA's educational literature such as the airplane flying handbook.

<u>NOTES:</u>

FORCED TO LAND AFTER ONGOING EQUIPMENT FAILURES

ASRS, 2018

During flight in IMC conditions on a segment of the IFR flight to ZZZ, the Mode "C" transponder began to display different types of altitude that was different from the altimeter.

Approach contacted me about the issue and I reset the transponder during the flight but that did not resolve the issue about the changing altitudes. When I pressed the PTT [Push To Talk] to advise Approach, the G430 screen reset itself during the flight.

In this particular aircraft, the G430 screen has the only communication radio and navigation radio in addition to the GPS equipment that I was using for the flight. After the GPS unit reset itself, I called Approach and told them the Mode C transponder was turned off and back on but the issue was not resolved.

Once again, I pushed the PTT button to transmit, the GPS screen turned off and remained off. Once this occurred, I made the decision to get out of IMC conditions so I descended to 3,500 feet into VFR conditions. At this point of the flight, I just passed ZZZ airport and I made a mental note of where the nearest airport was at.

Approach asked me where I was at in altitude and I told them I was 3,500 feet due to the GPS screen was not functioning properly and I was not going to be in IMC conditions with this issue.

I made up my mind that I did not want to continue the flight and I asked for a priority landing at ZZZ so that I can attempt to determine the problem or call the mechanic and explain the situation.

Approach either didn't hear my request or was too busy with other things, so I am not sure if my request was heard. I was able to communicate with Approach with a black screen on the GPS unit during this time.

About 2-3 minutes later, communication was lost with Approach and I was not able to hear them or talk. I told Approach I was cancelling the IFR flight plan and diverting to ZZZ for a landing. Another aircraft on the same frequency that I was on relayed from ZZZ Tower that I was cleared to land on any runway.

I relayed acknowledgement of the message and told the plane that I had limited to no communications and no GPS screen which has the communication and navigation radio channels. The other aircraft told me I was cleared to land on any runway, so I made a landing on RWY XX where I was met by the fire department and an Operations personnel.

I told them no one was injured, nor the aircraft, nor was there any fire or damage to the aircraft, just a communication and GPS screen issue.

I was escorted to the FBO by the Operations personnel where I made a phone call to the flight school and expressed the issues I had during the flight. I honestly don't know what caused the issue nor do I know what could have been done to prevent the issue from occurring in the future.

Lessons Learned:

I was heavily reliant on the G430 screen for communication and navigation.

When the screen malfunctioned, I was left without any backup options. It is important to have a backup plan in case of equipment failure, such as carrying a handheld radio or being familiar with alternative navigation methods. Have a backup plan.

When I noticed that there was a problem with the transponder and GPS screen, I made the decision to get out of IMC conditions and descend to VFR conditions. Always prioritize safety over completing the flight.

When I lost communication with ATC, I was able to utilize another aircraft on the same frequency to relay information.

NOTES:

TRIM CABLE HAD BEEN INSTALLED BACKWARDS

ASRS, 2014

My plan had me flying 15 miles away to pick up my son at another airport. I had filed an Instrument Flight Plan (IFP) to commence from the next airport after picking him up. However, about 30 seconds into my takeoff climb, I sensed the need to relieve nose down trim and turned the trim wheel slightly for nose up.

The nose down pressure worsened, and my initial thought was a stuck elevator. I visually checked and the elevator was moving properly. However, I was gaining airspeed but could not climb even though I had the yoke pulled back to my stomach with tremendous force required.

I trimmed a bit more and the problem worsened - I was now almost 'full' nose up trim with the yoke fully back. I was about to look for a place to put down as I didn't know how long I could hold the yoke back and knew landing was going to be very difficult. At this point, I was past the emergency landing field)

On a hunch, I turned the trim wheel the opposite direction - nose down - and immediately felt a relief of the pressure.

Further nose down trim relieved the nose down pressure. After some back and forth with the trim wheel, I realized that the trim cable had been installed/wound backward on the spool. By operating the trim opposite of normal, I was able to recover normal control, turn around and make a normal landing at the airport I had departed from.

Upon return I reported the incident to the Flight Chief. Recently the Operator had lost its Mechanic and had had [aircraft] firewall work done by a private aviation service on airport. Upon re-inspection, the Operator and Mechanic determined that the trim cable had been re-installed backward as part of the firewall work and I was the first person to fly the plane post-repair.

Lessons Learned:

I had checked both Manual and Electric Trim as part of the Pre-flight Checklist and took off with trim in "Takeoff" position. However, I now realize that the Preflight Checklist I used included a check that, Electric Trim was "in motion" when activated by the yoke-mounted button, but did not include noting a proper DIRECTION of motion. I have since added that check to my Pre-flight Checklist and have advised others to do so.

In talking to the Flight Chief, this is apparently something well known to Cessna mechanics, but an easy mistake for a less experienced mechanic to make.

NOTES:

OFF-FIELD LANDING DUE TO FLAP FAILURE

ASRS, 2019

Yesterday, I prepared to do some practice soft field TO/LDGs with my student, who is a very good student pilot. We checked the weather and saw no forecasted wind shear or anything that made me feel as if the flight was unsafe. We knew it had rained quite a bit recently, so before attempting the actual soft field, we overflew the airstrip and judged that it was dry enough in order to complete the tasks.

We began the flight by practicing 2 soft field takeoffs/landings at [the departure] airport. We then departed the area to the northeast, enroute to ZZZ airport. As stated earlier, we overflew the field and entered a teardrop into the left downwind for runway XX. We made UNICOM calls announcing our arrival and we heard no other aircraft in the vicinity.

Our approach was normal as expected. My student put full (40 degrees) flaps down (electrical flaps). We then encountered 2 cases of windshear and my student elected to make a Go-around and I agreed it was a good idea.

He added full power, turned the carb heat off and attempted to put the flaps up. I notice that the flap indicator hadn't moved and looked outside and realized we had a real problem. The flaps were stuck at 40 degrees.

At this time, I took control of the aircraft and focused solely on maintaining positive control of the aircraft. We struggled to maintain altitude and I recall seeing the VSI reading 0 while we were around 75-80 MPH. So, here we are, following the river at the same altitude as the ridge to our right with trees everywhere. I was very nervous at this point, but did my best to remain calm and control the aircraft as I had been trained to do.

We followed the river for about 1.5 NM and I planned to continue following it until we were able to climb or found somewhere to put it down safely. Around 1.5 NM south of ZZZ, I recall seeing the smoke stacks along the left side of the river. Further down the river, I saw power lines draped over the river at our altitude. I knew that we would not be able to make it over those. Moments later, I look to my right and see a break in the tree line over the ridge. Out of the grace of God, a corn field appeared that had a window of maybe .2 NM for me to shoot into it. I immediately began flying towards it.

Thankfully, I was able to successfully complete a safe landing. Neither my student nor I were injured to any degree, and the aircraft was in perfect conditions other than some mud and the flaps being stuck.

I then called my FBO and they sent the mechanic and 2 pilots out. The mechanic was able to diagnose and fix the problem, we contacted the land owner and he gave us permission to fly it out of the field. The other two pilots flew it back and my student and I rode back with the mechanic in his truck, as we were in shock from believing we might be going down just a couple hours prior.

My student did a great job calling out airspeed for me when needed and it definitely contributed to the success of our scenario. When I saw the corn field, I asked him if he thought we should land it. He said yes, and I agreed.

I was under very high pressure to fly the aircraft and knew I wouldn't be able to think 100% clearly so I decided to ask for his opinion even though he has limited experience. I learned that Crew Resource Management is a very effective tool, especially in high pressure situations such as this one yesterday.

Lessons Learned:

To my understanding, there was an electrical issue with the flaps that resulted in them not retracting properly. I assume it was due to wear and tear of this slightly older training aircraft.

I am very proud of my student for maintaining a calm, cool and collected demeanor during the entire event. Had he been freaking out, it may have caused me to as well and who knows what would have happened?

I am very proud of my piloting skills and quick decision making during this entire event as well. Together, we made the assessment that landing in the corn field was the best possible action and looking back, I still believe it.

NOTES:

OLD PHRASEOLOGY AND STICKY BUTTONS

ASRS, 2016

It was a beautiful clear fall day with unlimited visibility and high ceilings. I was in a Cessna 172 with G1000 avionics. I had requested clearance for a "Photo op" flight over the ZZZ Class C airspace.

ZZZ clearance cleared me for 2000 feet, was given a transponder code and the departure frequency. I am very familiar with my aircraft and I knew my COM frequency toggle key responds slowly and tends to stick a little, and you have to mash hard at times. So, when I set COM 1 for tower and departure frequencies; I had to mash the switch twice for the tower frequency to move to the active side.

Then I contacted Ground on COM 2 and taxied short of Runway XY. Then I pushed the dual COM knob to toggle up to COM 1 and contacted Tower, "ZZZ Tower, Skyhawk with you at XY with information Quebec."

Immediately I got a response, "Skyhawk state intention, altitude and position". The radios had a little squelch but still I was confused at the request.

Since the flight plan was an unusual request for a photo op which I have never done before, I assumed that he wanted to know exactly what I was doing. So I said "Skyhawk for a photo op at 2000 feet ready at Runway XY" OR at least that is what I thought I said.

When he came back with another transponder code, this really confused me but I complied. The second time I heard him say my call sign, and the word "position". I assumed he meant "Position and Hold" and looked both ways for traffic, there was no one on short final and I went ahead and lined up and waited. I was nervous that I may be holding up others. I was puzzled at his use of old terminology of "position (and hold)" instead of "line up and wait" but did not ask for clarification since I was convinced that I was talking to Tower.

By this time, I had a nagging feeling that something was amiss. I kept calling "Tower" with no response. I could see the Tower and I felt like waving to them to see if they forgot me. I had looked back and saw no one on short final. A few minutes felt like hours and how I wished that Cessna had installed a "reverse gear".

It never occurred to me that I was on the wrong frequency until the controller said, "Skyhawk contact tower". I looked up at COM 1, I was shocked and mortified to see that I was on departure frequency.

I think that the departure controller thought I was an incoming aircraft, and I thought I was talking to the tower because after I announced that I was holding short at XY, he did not correct me and I did not check to see that I was on the wrong frequency.

When I pushed the toggle key once, I should have waited for it to respond rather than push it again. The tower frequency briefly moved to active then moved back to standby and I did not notice the change.

I was completely in shock that this could happen to me. Tower instructed me to take [taxiway] off the active runway and contact ground, which I did. By now I was totally embarrassed and incoherent and I am sure I did not make any sense. He seemed genuinely puzzled when he asked me what happened. He asked me to contact the supervisor on a regular phone once I was on the ramp.

I thought I took all the right steps before the flight. I contacted the flight school where I trained and discussed with my instructors, I called ZZZ tower to inform of my intentions and ask for the optimal times to fly in class C airspace and the potential route and altitude. I checked the sectionals. I even had Foreflight loaded on my iPad.

There are several factors that in hindsight could have contributed to this. I spent too much time planning the flight to the point it was distracting. I thought I had enough sleep and was rested but probably not. I enjoy flying and feel very confident at the controls of my Cessna and was needlessly worrying about the fact that I will be weaving in and out of class C airspace because I wanted it just right.

The words "Position and Hold" are no longer used to instruct a pilot to enter the runway and await takeoff clearance. The new "Line Up and Wait" phraseology is used.

I trained [over 20 years ago] and after a gap of several years of minimal activity, had recently been flying a lot more and have not had many opportunities to "Line up and wait".

The chain of events heightening my anxiety, I misinterpreted the word "position" and had a knee jerk reaction due to years of using that terminology. This was compounded by the fact that I was convinced that I was talking to Tower.

Lessons Learned:

1. I could have asked for a safety pilot or an instructor for the practice "Photo Op" to avoid distractions. Once I was confident, I could have flown on my own the second time.
2. I find that a self-appraisal of "Am I safe to fly?" is not enough, I will use a check list next time. When you are at reduced performance, you are the worst person to judge this due to confirmation bias. I think a validated "performance questionnaire" may help.
3. My Cessna checklist doesn't specifically ask me to check on radio frequencies.

4. Although I have always checked frequencies I will now include it in writing in my checklist in all phases of flight.

5. Learn all the changes in ATC communication and if ANY doubt ask. Since then I have reviewed the videos from the FAA aviation safety website and AOPA on phraseology changes

6. If something does not feel right, it is not. Communication is most important, even if it is counterintuitive to your nature. If something sounds odd, rather than fear being embarrassed, ask for clarification. The entire conversation with "Tower" was strange and I should have asked for clarification rather than try to interpret or read between the lines.

NOTES:

CHAPTER 11

TECHNOLOGY & AUTOMATION

"It's just showing that no dream's impossible, that you can get out there and achieve anything if you put your mind to it."

Oliver O'Halloran
>   Youngest person to circumnavigate Australia
>   (solo and unassisted in a Cessna 172)
>   3 June 2017

LOSING GPS

ASRS, 2015

This was my first 2 hour cross-country out of state since earning my license a few months ago. I spent several nights flight planning and discussed the route with two other pilots.

After Takeoff, opened my flight plan, contacted local Bravo approach for transition and requested Flight Following. Transitioned the Bravo without incident, and was on flight following. Trip duration was 2.5 hours at 115kts. Several handoffs from FF, including military approach, all successful.

About 50 miles from destination I lost GPS signal, and every time I tried to pull up the electronic chart, it would default to the equator. Since I knew if I stayed on course the airport was on the other side of the Ridge some 30+ minutes away, and I was on FF if I needed help and the final handoff would mean I was about 20 minutes away.

I stopped trying to get the GPS signal back and setup the electronic chart just as a chart.

Shortly after losing GPS, FF stated the automatic handoff was not working and FF is now canceled and return to own VFR navigation.

Now I start to get pretty nervous, and I start to monitor ATIS. I see one of my waypoints to the right, and ATIS gets picked up. Once I have ATIS I call the Tower, still do not see the ridge (airport is on the other side of the ridge) and report I am some 30+ miles out. They say to report when I am closer.

Getting more nervous, I see the ridge and start my descent from 8,500 to below 8000. I call Tower again and report I'm xx miles from the airport, they reply that I must be too low because they do not see me on radar.

Slowly descending but not too much so I have proper terrain avoidance over the ridge but more nervous because I start to question my Altimeter because Tower just told me I was too low. I call Tower and tell them I can't be too low because I am at 8,500. I was already below 8,000 but reported where I was just 2 minutes ago which was 8,500. They go on to tell me I am in the Bravo without clearance, and still not on radar. Now I busted Bravo, Tower is telling me I am too low, the ridge is fast approaching at 5,500, FF dropped me 10 minutes ago and GPS is down.

I get over the ridge, I don't remember my altitude at this point, but I don't think I was in the Bravo because I was able to get to traffic pattern altitude pretty quickly after going over the ridge.

Tower has me circle twice then cleared for RW 17L. I enter left base, wide turn to final for 17L, over 17L (too high) Tower yells at me that I was cleared for 17L. I think he means I am over the taxiway or on the wrong RW so I go around. Very high anxiety at this point, I'm told to make left traffic, which I do and land without incident. Tower tells me to turn on E, stay on this frequency and stop between the runways. I do. Hhe gives me a number, then tells me to cross runway 17R and contact ground.

I cross the RW, the taxiway is right in front of me and parking is just a few feet away, I turn to my left and see a plane taxing towards me so I full throttle to get out of the runway environment.

At that moment I questioned the instructions from Tower, I must have heard them wrong, the safest thing was not to be where I was. I'm out of the RW environment. Tower continues to rightfully yell at me, I struggle to change radios but finally get a hold of ground where they say parking is to my left.

I depart that airport a few hours later and return home via several Bravo/Military transitions without incident.

Lessons Learned:

Once home, I spend the next hour going through everything to find out what I did wrong and how it could have been avoided.

1. I should have planned on going around the Ridge, since the bottom shelf of the Bravo and the top of the Ridge were too close for my experience level.
2. Needed to trust my Altimeter because it was properly updated the entire trip and could not be off as much as I started to think.
3. Do not rely on the GPS, I may not have known the exact miles or minutes from the airport but I knew the direction and final way point.
4. Stopping before the taxiway would have been a safe, and correct choice as well.

The next day I attended a FAAST seminar, contacted my CFI for some additional ground discussion and practice flight training on entering the airport environment from a high altitude with Bravo transitions. I don't think I busted the Bravo, and as far as I know I was never on radar because I was too low. I'm also reviewing airport signs and procedures since not stopping short of the hold line Taxiway and contacting ground was my biggest concern.

NOTES:

IPAD FAILURE

ASRS, 2015

Before departure, I did my typical run-up procedures, instrument checks, etc., and got set up with my Garmin 650 GPS for the LOC Runway 2 approach into WVI. I did this on the ground to reduce my workload in the air for this lesson.

After completing all my tasks, I then took off and departed downwind and began my set up for the approach. I have an XGPS 160 that links with my iPad (wifi only) so that I can see my position inflight and record my progress.

As I was starting my approach briefing and setup, demonstrating to my CFII, my iPad was not allowing me to activate my approach plates. This was discovered midflight upon reaching my cruising altitude of 4,500 feet. We were going to be getting Pop-Up IFR clearance since we were approaching MVFR to IMC conditions due to the marine layer coming in.

From my interpretation, I had believed all maps and charts would be up to date since they changed the day before.

It appeared that the maps that I thought had been updated overnight had actually not been downloaded on my iPad and my maps, approaches, and terminal procedures were all inaccessible. I should add this in my preflight check.

After this was discovered, I didn't say anything to my CFII and instead decided to remove the iPad from my yoke mount and throw it in the back since it was no longer useful to me.

Since I am getting ready for my check ride soon, I decided to treat myself as if it were me solo in an IFR flight and grabbed a spare set of instrument charts in a Terminal Procedure book I had in hand in case of this very situation. I also had a paper enroute chart and all the charts downloaded on my iPhone as a worst case scenario.

To give myself more time with the paper charts and to still maintain my flight I just powered back to 55% power to not rush and handle the situation.

After I had the paper charts, I was able to successfully shoot 3 instrument approaches at night and luckily get some good practice basically simulation being alone in IFR condition. ATC was not notified since the issue was resolved with the paper charts.

Lessons Learned:

This isn't the first situation where this sort of event happened, another time happened when the temperature was 100+ and my iPad shutdown midflight during an ILS approach.

Again, paper charts are always a good resort.

Human Factors: human error, workload increase, fatigue, had a CFII as back up, didn't need to use

<u>NOTES:</u>

GLOSSARY
AVIATION TERMS

With hundreds (or thousands) of different aeronautical terms and abbreviations, we cannot begin to cover them all. Below are the most common terms:

A

Absolute Altitude – The vertical distance between the aircraft and ground level.

Absolute Ceiling – The highest altitude an aircraft can fly at maximum throttle while maintaining level height and constant airspeed.

Accelerated Stall – A stall that occurs at a higher airspeed than a normal stall due to a higher load factor (g).

ACFT – Aircraft.

ACM — Air Combat Maneuvering (also known as or dogfighting).

ADF — Automatic Direction Finder – A navigation system that identifies the relative bearing of an aircraft based on a radio beacon transmitting in the MF or LF bandwidth.

ADI — Attitude direction indicator.

Adiabatic Lapse Rate – The rate at which temperature changes due to increasing and decreasing altitude, under conditions of thermal equilibrium.

ADIZ — Air Defense Identification Zone – The airspace over both water and land within which the identification, location, and control of civil aircraft is required in the interest of national security.

Adverse Yaw – When an aircraft turns in the opposite direction of a roll due to use of ailerons and the difference in lift and drag of each wing.

AFB – Air Force Base.

AGL – Above Ground Level – The vertical distance measured between the aircraft and a specific land mass.

AIM — Aeronautical Information Manual – An official Federal Aviation Administration (FAA) publication that details proper pilot operation within the US National Airspace System, including Air Traffic Control (ATC) and aviation safety.

Aileron – The movable, hinged flight control surfaces that are used in pairs with opposite motions to control the roll of an aircraft.

Airfoil – The cross-sectional shape of a wing, blade, turbine, or rotor that produces lift.

Air Taxi Operator – An aircraft company that operates under FAR Part 135. The aircraft must be originally designed to have no more than 60 passenger seats or a cargo payload of 18,000 lbs and carries cargo or mail on either a scheduled or charter basis, and/or carries passengers on an on-demand basis or limited scheduled basis.

Altimeter – An instrument that measures an object's altitude above a fixed surface.

Altitude Indicator – An instrument that indicates aircraft orientation relative to earth's horizon.

AMT – Aviation Maintenance Technician, which is another term for an aircraft mechanic.

Angle of Attack – The angle between a reference line on an airfoil and the direction of the oncoming air.

Angle of Incidence – The angle at which a reference line on an airfoil is perpendicular to the aircraft's longitudinal surface axis.

Anhedral – The downward angle of aircraft wings from the horizontal cross-section of the wings.

Annual Inspection – A required aircraft inspection every 12 calendar months.

Apron – The paved area at an airport where aircraft park, fuel, load, and unload.

ASI — Air Speed Indicator – A pitot-static flight instrument that indicates airspeed of an aircraft through an air mass in miles per hour, knots, or both.

ATC — Air Traffic Control – A ground-based service that ensures safety of air traffic by directing aircraft in the area during take-off, landing, and while flying in the designated airspace.

ATIS — Automatic Terminal Information Service – A continuous broadcast of pre-recorded aviation information available to pilots around specific terminals. The information is constantly updated and designed for mass spreading of relevant information, which is particularly useful at busy airports.

Avionics Master Switch – A single switch that controls the electrical power for an aircraft's electronic communication and navigation instruments.

B

Base Leg – The flight path in an airport pattern that runs in the runway landing direction.

Best Lift Over Drag Ratio – Often referred to as 'L over D Max', this is the highest value of ratios of lift to drag for any airfoil.

BFM — Basic Fighter Maneuvers.

Blade Angle – The angle between the reference line of a propeller blade and a plane perpendicular to the axis of rotation.

Bleed Air – Hot compressed air produced during the compressor stage of aircraft engine operation.

C

C4ISR – Command, Control, Communications, Computers, Intelligence, Surveillance, and Reconnaissance Calibrated Airspeed – The indicated airspeed corrected for position and instrument error.

Camber – The convexity of curve on an aircraft wing.

Cargo – Goods carried on an aircraft.

CAVU — Ceiling and Visibility Unlimited – Describes ideal flying conditions with visibility of 10 or more miles and ceiling of at least 10,000 feet.

CAST – Combat Airman Skills Training.

CDI — Course Deviation Indicator – A navigational instrument that displays the lateral course deviation. When the aircraft is flying left of the selected course, the needle deflects proportionally to the right. When the aircraft is flight right of the selected course, the needle deflects proportionally to the left.

Ceiling – The height of the lowest cloud layer or obscuring phenomena that is reported as "broken", "overcast", or "obscuration", and not classified as "thin" or "partial".

CFI — Chief Flying Instructor.

CG — Center of Gravity – The longitudinal and lateral point over which the aircraft would balance.

Charter – The business of renting all seats on an aircraft rather than a commercial flight where seats are sold individually.

Chord Line – The imaginary straight line running between the airfoil's leading and trailing edges.

Clearance – The authorization provided by air traffic control for aircraft to proceed with a particular action in controlled airspace, which is designed to prevent aircraft collisions.

Climb – The act of increasing aircraft altitude, typically to a designated level.

CTAF — Common Traffic Advisory Frequency – A radio frequency used for air-to-air communication, allowing continued aircraft operation at non-towered airports or outside of tower operating hours.

Commuter – An aircraft category outlined by the FAA as "limited to propeller-driven, multi-engine airplanes that have a seating configuration, excluding pilot seats, of 19 or less, and a maximum certificated takeoff weight of 19,000 pound or less. The commuter category operation is limited to any maneuver incident to normal flying, stalls (except whip stalls), and steep turns, in which the angle of bank is not more than 60 degrees.".

Constant-Speed Propeller – A propeller designed to maintain a consistent engine RPM by automatic increases and decreases of the blade pitch.

Contrail – A streak of condensed water vapor in the air due to the heat produced by aircraft engines at high altitudes.

Controlled Airspace – Designated airspace within which Air Traffic Control provides aircraft movement instructions and regulations.

Crosswind – Wind that is blowing perpendicular to the aircraft course.

D

Descent – The act of decreasing aircraft altitude, typically to a designated level.

DME — Distance Measuring Equipment – Radio navigation technology used to measure the distance between the aircraft and a ground station.

Distress – An internationally-recognized signal for danger and need for immediate assistance.

Downwind Leg – A flight path parallel to but running the opposite direction of the runway intended for landing.

Drag – A parallel and opposing force to an aircraft's motion through the air.

E

Elevator – Horizontal surfaces that control aircraft pitch and are typically hinged to the stabilizer.

Empennage – Another phrase for the tail of an aircraft, which provides stability during flight.

ETA — Estimated Time of Arrival – The time you will arrive at a destination, based on the local time.

ETE — Estimated Time en Route – The amount of time you will spend traveling to a destination.

F

FAA — Federal Aviation Administration.

FBO — Fixed Base Operator – An organization at an airport that offers aviation services, such as hangar, parking, and tie-down space; airplane maintenance and rentals; and fuel.

Feathering – The act of adjusting variable pitch propellers so that the blades are in line with airflow and overall drag is reduced.

Ferry Flight – A flight intended to return an aircraft to base; deliver a new aircraft from the manufacturer to the purchaser; move an aircraft from one operations base to another; or moving an aircraft for the purpose of maintenance.

Final Approach – A flight path running in the direction of the runway intended for landing that ends with a landing.

Firewall – A fire-resistant bulkhead that is situated between the engine and other aircraft areas.

Flaps – Flaps are a kind of high-lift device used to increase the lift of an aircraft wing at a given airspeed. Flat devices, typically located on the edges of a an aircraft wing, that control lift at specific speeds.

Flare – A maneuver that typically occurs during the landing stage of an aircraft. The aircraft nose is pointed upwards, which lowers the descent rate in preparation for landing.

Flight Deck – An area at the front of airplane where the pilot and aircraft controls are situated.

Flight Plan – Formatted information provided by pilots or dispatchers regarding an upcoming flight, including details such as destination, path, timing, etc.

FLIR — Forward-looking infrared camera.

Fuselage – The central portion of an aircraft, which is intended to house the flight crew, passengers, and cargo.

G

General Aviation – The division of civil aviation aircraft operations that includes all but commercial air transport and aerial work.

Glass Cockpit – A term used to describe an aircraft that is fully equipped with electronic, digital flight instrument displays, instead of analog-style gauges.

GLOC — G-force induced loss of consciousness.

Gross Weight – The aircraft weight including people, cargo, fuel, etc.

Ground Effect – The increasing lift and decreasing drag that occurs as a result of an aircraft's wings as it gets closer to the ground.

Groundspeed – The horizontal speed of an aircraft relative to the surface below.

H

Hangar – A building made to hold aircraft for storing, maintenance, assembly, etc.

HOCAS — Hands-on collective and stick.

Horizontal Stabilizer – The horizontal stabilizer prevents up-and-down, or pitching, motion of the aircraft nose.

Hypoxia – A condition caused by low levels of oxygen that can lead to dizziness, disorientation, etc, posing extreme danger to pilots operating aircraft at high altitudes.

I

IAS — Indicated Airspeed – The speed of an aircraft displayed on the airspeed indicator, which is determined by the pitot-static tube and does not take into account any outside factors.

IFR — Instrument Flight Rules – Regulations that define aircraft operations when pilots are not able to operate using visual references.

ILS — Instrument Landing System – A ground-based system that provides directional information for aircraft attempting to land in low visibility situations.

IMC — Instrument Meteorological Conditions – Weather conditions that describe a situation where pilots are not able to operate using visual references.

J

Joystick – The control column in the aircraft is often called a joystick. It is the main device that controls the aircraft and is typically mounted on the ceiling or floor if the aircraft has a joystick instead of a yoke.

K

Knot – A measurement of speed that takes into account nautical miles: 1 knot = 1 nautical mile per hour = 6076 feet per hour. 1 mph =1 mile per hour = 5280 feet per hour.

L

Laminar-Flow Airfoil – The smooth airflow over an aircraft wing with minimized drag.

LANTIRN — Low Altitude Navigation and Targeting Infrared for Night — a combined navigation and targeting pod system used on the USAF's premier fighter aircraft.

Lift – The force that directly opposes aircraft weight, generated primarily by the wings.

Load Factor (g) – The smooth airflow over an aircraft wing with minimized drag.

Longitudinal Axis – The directional that runs horizontally from the aircraft nose to tail.

M

Mach – The ratio of aircraft speed to the speed of sound through the medium where the aircraft is traveling.

Magnetic Compass – The directional orientation of an aircraft according to the geomagnetic field.

Magnetic Deviation – The error produced by the unavoidable magnetic impact of aircraft materials.

Magnetic North – Unlike the geographical north (North Pole), this point is the location indicated as North by where the compass points.

Magneto – An aircraft engine component that generates high voltage to ignite spark plugs.

METAR – A pilot weather report delivered on a continuous basis.

MSL — Mean Sea Level – The average level of the surface an ocean used as a basis for vertical measurements.

N

NATOPS — Naval Aviation Training and Operating Procedures Standardization Manual.

NOTAMs – Abbreviation for "Notices to airmen." — written notices provided to pilots prior to flights advising them of relevant circumstances.

NTSB — National Transportation Safety Board.

NVG – Night Vision Goggles.

O

OG – Operations Group.

Operating Limitations – Restrictions defined by an aircraft manufacturer including airspeed, weight, etc.

Overshoot – Landing aircraft beyond the runway.

P

PAX – Air passengers.

Payload – The weight of the content carried in an aircraft, including passengers, pilots, cargo, etc.

PFD — Primary Flight Display – The main screen used by pilots in aircraft containing an electronic flight instrument system.

PIC — Pilot in Command – The designated individual that is responsible for safe aircraft operations during flight.

Pitch – The movement of an aircraft, characterized by the nose and tail rising and falling.

Pitot Tube – A small device located on the front outside edge of an airfoil, used to measure air pressure.

Propeller – A piece of aircraft equipment that contains rotating blades, creating engine thrust.

Q

QHI — Qualified helicopter instructor.

Quadraplane – An aircraft that has 4 wings of the same size.

R

RAF – Royal Air Force.

RESA — Runway End Safety Area – A surface located beyond the runway designated as a place for aircraft to enter in an attempt to minimize risk during unplanned occurrences, such as an overshoot.

RLG — Relief landing ground.

Roll – Aircraft rotation along the longitudinal axis, which runs from the nose to tail.

RPM — Revolutions per minute of the engine.

Rudder – An aircraft surface used to control the yaw movement.

Runway – A "defined rectangular area on a land aerodrome prepared for the landing and takeoff of aircraft".

RVR — Runway visual range.

S

Short Field – A runway that is shorter in length and requires aircraft to minimize the amount of runway used when taking off or landing.

Sideslip – An aircraft movement that typically aligns with the lateral force of the wind and results in a sideways flow.

Skid – The sliding and outward pivoting movement of the aircraft that occurs as a result of a shallow turn.

Slip – The sliding and inward pivoting movement of the aircraft that occurs as a result of a steep turn.

Soft Field – A runway that is not paved and made of elements such as dirt or grass.

Squawk – A four-digit code given to an aircraft by ATC to allow for simple identification of an aircraft in a given region.

Stall – The condition that occurs as a result of an aircraft exceeding its angle of attack and therefore experiencing decreased lift.

Standard Rate Turn – A turn that an aircraft makes at a rate of 3°/second or a 360° turn in two minutes.

Straight-and-Level Flight – Maintaining a consistent heading and altitude during flight.

T

Tail – The rear aircraft structure that provides aerodynamic stability.

Tarmac – The paved area at an airport where aircraft park, fuel, load, and unload.

Threshold – The area of a runway, designated with particular markings, indicating the beginning of a runway.

Throttle – A device that controls the amount of power outputted by the engine.

Thrust – A force which opposes aircraft drag and is created by the engines to propel the aircraft forward.

Torque – A force that is intended to produce rotation.

Touch-and-Go – An aircraft maneuver used to practice landing techniques by simply landing on the runway and taking off once more without coming to a full stop.

Transponder – An electronic device on airplanes that generate an output code, which is used for ATC identification purposes.

Trim Tab – Small surfaces on the trailing edge of a bigger control surface used to counteract the aerodynamic forces on the bigger control surface.

True Airspeed – The speed of an aircraft is the speed corrected for the errors caused by altitude and temperature.

True Altitude – The vertical height of an aircraft above Mean Sea Level (MSL).

Turbulence – A sudden violent shift in air flow caused by irregular atmospheric motion.

U

UAV – Unmanned Aerial Vehicle.

Upwind Leg – The flight path in an airport pattern that runs parallel to the runway landing direction, along the same direction the aircraft will be landing.

USAF - United States Air Force.

Useful Load – The weight of the items that can be taken out of the aircraft, including fuel, passengers, cargo, pilots, etc.

UTC – Universal Coordinated Time.

V

Vario — Variometer – a flight instrument used to inform the pilot of the rate of descent or climb.

VFR — Visual Flight Rules – Regulations that define aircraft operations when pilots are able to operate using visual references.

VFR On Top – The condition where IFR conditions exist, however VFR conditions exact above the cloud layer.

VHF – Very High Frequency Omni-Directional Range.

VMC — Visual Meteorological Conditions – Weather conditions that describe a situation where pilots are able to operate using visual references.

VOR – A short-range radio aircraft navigation system that allows equipped aircraft to receive directional information through radio signals from ground-based beacons.

VORTAC — a radio-based navigational aid for aircraft pilots consisting of a co-located VHF omnidirectional range beacon and a tactical air navigation system beacon.

VSI — Vertical Speed Indicator – A device that provides the feet per minute (fpm) rate at which an aircraft is climb or descending.

W

WAG – Wild-ass guess.

Weight-Shift-Control – A method used by pilots to steer a hang glider or paraglider whereby they push a control bar attached to the wing structure.

Wind Shear – An abrupt change in horizontal or vertical wind direction.

Y

Yaw – The movement of an aircraft, characterized by the nose moving side-to-side.

Yoke – The aircraft control devices used by pilot for changes in attitude, as well as pitch and roll movement.

Y-plane – Prototype aircraft.

Z

Zoomie – Nickname for an Air Force Academy graduate or cadet.

Zulu Time – A term synonymous with UTC (Universal Coordinated Time), which is the same as Greenwich Mean Time. Pilots file all flight plans in Zulu Time.

ACKNOWLEDGMENTS

I want to thank the people who have helped with my flying career. Whether they realise it or not, our fun conversations or serious chats, and all the discussions around flying have helped immeasurably with these books. Thank you. You will probably never realise how many lives you have saved by inspiring me to publish these books.

ABOUT THE AUTHOR

With a passion for aviation, Fletcher first flew solo in a glider at the age of 16, then tried parachuting several dozen times, before graduating onto paragliding, then finally obtaining his Private Pilots License.

He is the producer of the global television show "FlightPathTV" which is on air in over 60 countries, and travels extensively interviewing pilots from around the world whilst filming the world's leading air shows.

Coupled with twenty years of experience working with global entrepreneurs through EO (Entrepreneurs Organisation), training them to experience share between each other and to learn from any mistakes, Fletcher selected and compiled these stories to help us learn from others. To ensure current and future pilots will be safe in the skies.

www.fletchermckenzie.com